Books by John White

THE COST OF COMMITMENT
DARING TO DRAW NEAR
EROS DEFILED
EXCELLENCE IN LEADERSHIP
THE FIGHT
FLIRTING WITH THE WORLD
THE GOLDEN COW
HEALING THE WOUNDED (with Ken Blue)
THE MASKS OF MELANCHOLY
PARABLES (LifeGuide Bible Study)
PARENTS IN PAIN
PUTTING THE SOUL BACK IN PSYCHOLOGY
THE RACE
WHEN THE SPIRIT COMES WITH POWER

The Archives of Anthropos by John White

THE TOWER OF GEBURAH
THE IRON SCEPTRE
THE SWORD BEARER

Booklets by John White

BIBLE STUDY
PRAYER

JOHN WHITE

PARENTS IN PAIN

Overcoming the Hurt & Frustration of Problem Children

INTERVARSITY PRESS
DOWNERS GROVE, ILLINOIS 60515

InterVarsity Press is the book-publishing division of Inter-Varsity Christian Fellowship, a student movement active on campus at hundreds of universities, colleges and schools of nursing. For information about local and regional activities, write IVCF, 233 Langdon St., Madison, WI 53703.

Distributed in Canada through InterVarsity Press, 1875 Leslie St., Unit 10, Don Mills, Ontario M3B 2M5, Canada.

All Bible quotations, unless otherwise indicated, are from the Revised Standard Version of the Bible, copyrighted 1946, 1952, © 1971 and 1973.

ISBN 0-87784-582-4
Library of Congress Catalog Card Number: 78-24760

Printed in the United States of America

18   17   16   15   14   13   12   11
93   92   91   90   89   88

To John René

Prolog

*H*oney, a police car just pulled in front of the house."

Jim and Elaine stared at it, ominous even without flashing lights. A couple of bystanders stopped to watch along with some neighborhood children. Curtains across the street were slowly drawn aside.

For a minute nothing happened.

Then from the car emerged two uniformed city police officers. One of them held the door open to allow a bedraggled youth to get out.

"Peter!" Elaine said hoarsely. Yet she was not surprised. She had long feared this very scene.

Slowly Peter, his head held high and defiant, walked up the path between the two officers. Jim and Elaine felt suspended in a foreign universe. Yet when the trio finally reached the front door, the bell sounded with unnatural clarity.

"Oh, God!" Elaine said softly. "What do we do now?"

It was a girl's voice on the phone.

"Mr. Blackwell? It's Joanie....You know, Joanie, Cathy's friend."

"Yes, Joanie?"

"Well, Cathy's ... she's ill—I mean, she's been drinking, like. She's lying in the snow. She won't get up. I'm awfully sorry, Mr. Blackwell."

"Where are you?"

"I'm calling from the Seven-Eleven store on the corner of Osborne and River."

"Is that where she is?"

"Well, she's outside. Could you come and get her?" The girl's voice was shaking.

Rod Blackwell sighed.

"I'll be right over, Joanie."

At first when he arrived he could see only Joanie under a street lamp. As he parked the car and crossed the street he did not immediately discover where Cathy was. Joanie came to meet him.

"Where is she?"

Joanie pointed. The snow bank was in the shadow of a tall wall, and still he did not see until he was within six feet of them.

There were three huddled figures—two teen-age boys and Cathy, half sitting, half lying in the snow. As he leaned over her he smelled rye whiskey and vomit. He pulled her by her shoulders into a sitting position. "Hey! C'mon, Cathy! Get on your feet!"

Cathy's head lolled sideways. Mucus drooled from her mouth. "Can't. . . . "

"Give me a hand, Joanie. We can walk her over to the car, I think."

He sat beside her, hooked her left arm around his shoulders and hoisted her to her feet. Joanie supported her from the other side. Rod half dragged, half threw her into the front seat. She huddled against it, coughed and vomited. She was wet and shivering. Rod closed the door making sure first that her feet were inside.

"How much have they had?"

"I'm not sure. Jim got it from the liquor store. He looks eighteen."

"You must know *about* how much."

"Well, we had two fifty-two-ounce bottles of Gimli Goose (that's the cheapest wine we could get) and a twenty-six of rye."

"Is it all gone?"

The girl nodded.

"Who drank most?"

She shook her head. "I'm not sure. I had some too, but I don't like it."

"Who's Jim?"

"I don't know his family name. He lives in East Kildonan."

"And the other guy?"

"That's Brad Friesen. His folks go to your church."

He stood for a second. Hospital? They'd have to wait for hours in the emergency room. Some newly graduated casualty officer would give Cathy a sloppy examination and throw her out when her head began to clear. Rage was boiling inside Rod's body—rage, shame, disgust . . . and pity.

"Mr. Blackwell."

"Yes, Joanie?"

"I don't know what to do with the boys."

He paused and thought.

"Let's shove them into the back seat. Could you sit with them?"

She nodded.

"D'you know where Jim lives?"

Again she nodded.

"It's just around the corner from the Friesens'. I live right near there."

Half an hour later they propped Brad against the Friesens' front door, rang the bell, went back to the car and got inside. As they saw the door open, Rod eased the car gently up the street. He was in no mood to meet Brad's parents tonight.

Jim seemed to be coming out of it.

"I'll take him in," Joanie volunteered. "There's a light on in the living room. There must be someone at home. I can walk home from there."

She and Rod stood Jim on his feet, placing his arm round Joanie's neck.

"S'aw right. I c'n walk. 'M not drunk."

Joanie steered Jim toward the gap in the snow bank. As Rod got back into the driver's seat he heard Joanie say, "Thank you, Mr. Blackwell. An' I really am sorry about what happened."

All the way home Cathy sniveled between her coughs and shivers. "I'm sorry, daddy. I know I'm drunk. Don' be mad at me, daddy.... Oh, daddy, *please* don' be mad at me. I din' wanna hurt you. I *really* di'n't wanna hurt you an' I've done it again."

As he weaved his way homeward through the city traffic, Rod sighed again. *In vino veritas?* He knew that tomorrow she would again be the arrogant, defiant daughter he had grown so used to.

She found his young body hanging from a rafter in the basement. She dropped her basket of clothes, letting them scatter over the floor, as she ran to cut him down. Then she scrabbled with her long nails to get the rope from round his neck.

"My baby. Oh, my baby!" She sobbed dryly without any tears. Sitting cross-legged on the floor, cradling his stiff shoulders and head on her lap, she rocked herself backward and forward. Twenty minutes must have passed before she saw the note.

"I'm sorry, mom and dad," it read. "I *do* love you. I know you think I don't, but I do. I didn't want to mess things up. Every time I try I just go down the hole. Tell the other kids I love them. I'm sorry I've bungled it all up. It'll all be over now.

Give my guitar to Stan and my radio to Susan. I want dad to have my Bible. I read it this morning, but it doesn't make sense anymore. I want mom to wear my ring. *Please,* mom.

"I'm doing this because everything is black. I won't be able to hurt anyone anymore now."

But the hurt had scarcely begun.

Mary always jumped when the telephone rang. She'd been doing it for over six months. This time she was especially edgy since her daughter Renée had been out all night. Renée was just fourteen.

"Hello. Is that Mrs. Gray?" It was a boy's voice.

"Speaking."

"Er, . . . I'm . . . er, . . . I'm just calling about Renée."

"Who's speaking?"

"A friend."

"But what friend? Who are you? Where is she?"

"She said to say she was all right an' you musn't worry."

"But where *is* she?"

There was a pause.

"Well, . . . like I don't know."

"Is she staying with someone?"

"No." The answer came without hesitation.

"Then what?"

"She said to say she was going away."

"Going away? Going away where?"

"I dunno. To Vancouver mebbe."

"But she had no money. How could she go to Vancouver?" The boy's voice was scared.

"She said to say she was all right. That's all she said. Mrs. Gray, I gotta go to class now."

There was a click and the phone went dead.

Mary stood for a minute, still holding the phone in her hand. Then she dropped it and ran upstairs calling, "Gerry! Gerry! Gerry! She's *gone,* Gerry. She's run away! *Gerry?*"

Some parents don't care. They've learned to live with it or to shrug it off. But thousands, perhaps millions, are being torn. Their pain is the worse because many of them have a need to cover their tragedy. Appearances are more important to some parents than to others. You notice that church dignitaries and political figures tend to hide their family tragedies, facing the world behind masks.

Bewildered, angry, hurt, guilt-ridden, asking themselves a hundred questions to which there seem to be no answers, many parents just want to know how to make it through the next twenty minutes. Some walk through life with a burden that grows no lighter with the passage of time. Others are beaten into despair. If there is a quietness in their souls, it is the quietness of hopes that have died. Indeed they carefully refuse themselves hope, for hope is the harbinger of pain.

Are you a parent in pain? I cannot promise to heal you, but there is ease in sharing pain. Many parents have shared with me. Some have written their stories and allowed me to relate them in these pages. Names and certain facts have been changed to protect their privacy. But the essentials remain that others might be comforted.

My object in writing is to come to the rescue of parents. It is only incidentally to deal with child rearing. Books on how to bring up children from birth through college are ten a penny. Yet all the books on child rearing have not stopped the flood of adolescent problems and tragedies. What is needed is something to help parents in anguish to grapple with their distresses and to find hope in their despair. I want this to be such a book.

Although I am a practicing psychiatrist my confidence does not spring from any psychiatric expertise. For I am also a practicing father, one who has made mistakes, who has struggled at times with a sense of hopeless inadequacy and who has grappled with the shame and the pain about one of his five children who went astray. I have known a sickening dread when police cars drew up to my house and men in blue walked up the path to the front door. I have known wakeful nights, rages, bitterness, frustration, shame, futile hopes being shattered and the cruel battle between tenderness and contempt.

Lorrie and I had no idea what we were in for when we got married. We *thought* we were aware that family life would never be a bed of roses. For myself I was proud about entertaining no preconceived notions on how to bring up children and that I never criticized other people's child-rearing practices. *I* was not going to have anything to unlearn when *I* became a parent. Yet neither of us anticipated the long series of jolts and joys, ecstasies and agonies that awaited us. My "open-mindedness" was full of delusions, of false expectations and of unproved assumptions.

We thought we knew our strengths and weaknesses. We were modest. Indeed we were humble. As Christians we talked about our total inability to run our lives apart from God, and we thought we understood what we were saying. Christ would be at the center of *our* marriage. At the same time, with pious naiveté I imagined that such an intelligent spiritual husband with such a beautiful wife would undoubtedly give rise to four children (we planned four but the last one turned out to be twins) who would be the envy of parents everywhere.

As matters turned out it was Lorrie and I who were startled. As the years passed we grew progressively more humiliated and hurt. We little foresaw the day when we would sit in mutual pain, both of us silent because we had nothing left to say.

But if we had our lives to live over again we would not have it different. For in months and years of darkness we learned lessons we could never have learned in the light. Our souls have been stretched so that they now have a capacity for both joy and suffering that they never had before. The pain that could have shriveled and embittered us has made us stronger, more alive.

We have found God in a way and to a degree we never did before. We have found that he too is a parent who is willing to share the secrets of all parenting, who in fact invented the very institution. He knows more than the experts. In him we found healing and peace. By him we learned day by day how to cope with impossible problems. Through him our marriage is more solid than ever. He taught us what praying for our children was all about, what we could pray and what we couldn't.

We still are learning and we have more learning to do. But we would be selfish to keep our joys and solace to ourselves. They need to be shared as widely as possible. I write about them with the prayer that they will heal parents in pain, and if it shall so please God, restore many of their children, however impossible the situation might seem right now.

Toward that end I have organized this book in three parts. Part one considers why child rearing has become such a complicated task and how common sense, science and the Bible can help us sort it out. Part two centers on the parent-child relationship proper as trust erodes, arguments arise, and the need for professional and legal counsel develop. Part three amplifies the theme: as Christians we are called not to do what works but to do what is right. We are to follow the biblical injunctions not to pretend we own our children, but to discipline them and pray for them despite what we may consider to be undesirable results.

You may open my book wherever you will. Some parts may not be helpful to you, but other parts will be. It was designed for you. Though your bitterness may not allow you to see this at present, I want you to know that there is a God of all comfort who holds out to you the wine of truth.

I

It Ain't That Simple

1
The Age of Uncertainty

*U*ntil the twentieth century parents *knew* how to bring up their children. That is not to say they had no problems or even that they knew what they were doing. But by and large they had fewer misgivings and uncertainties than modern parents.

The Virtue of Stability

Tradition decreed how children should be reared. You brought them up in the no-nonsense way in which you yourself were raised—the way everybody brought up their children. Not all parents adhered to the tradition. Many suffered the griefs we still suffer today. Some were overindulgent, others unnecessarily harsh. But parents before the twentieth century were not harassed by the same anxieties about their roles as we are. If their children turned out badly, they were more inclined than we to blame the children and not themselves.

By the end of the nineteenth century, science had come to the rescue of many of us who until that point did not know we needed rescuing. The behavioral sciences told us what bad parents we had been. Bed wetting, temper tantrums, lying, stealing, adolescent turmoil, rebellion, nightmares, truanting from school, nail biting, smoking, drinking, masturbation and a host of other ills were either the result of faulty parenting or of normal things that parents should turn a blind eye to. Each kind of behavior had its own scientific explanation.

Suddenly we understood everything about the developing human organism. Parents could eat of the tree of knowledge (was it not good to look at and to be desired to make us all wise?), but to our dismay we found ourselves turned out of our parental garden (never really an Eden but tolerable nonetheless) into a cold and hostile world. The ground began to produce thorns and thistles, and by the sweat of our souls we reared our families.

A number of uncertainties plagued us. For one thing, child-rearing experts did not always agree. Popular articles in women's magazines explained opposing principles with equal lucidity and equal conviction. We were stripped of our naive confidence only to be handed confusing and conflicting advice.

About some things the advice *was* initially consistent. The earliest articles told us we were too punitive, too strict. The age of permissiveness dawned. Our children needed to express themselves, and express themselves they did. In some families parental tyranny was replaced by child tyranny, so that the latter estate was worse than the first.

But before long emphases began to shift as newer theories amended the defects of the old. We had ditched tradition and looked to science which meant that we had ditched something constant and understandable for something that was ever changing.

Whether tradition was right or wrong, it had the virtue of being stable. You knew where you were with tradition. If someone asked you why you did something a certain way, you simply said, "Because that's the proper way to do it." But with science you can be sure of nothing. Yesterday's "assured findings" will be tossed out tomorrow. No sooner have you begun to get the hang of a theory than someone comes to tell you that your theory is now known to be wrong. To your dismay you discover that instead of helping your children you have been harming them. However, all is not lost. The damage done by the old theory can be remedied by the new. But who is to say that the latest theory will not be replaced by yet another tomorrow?

A Deeper Uncertainty

There is a deeper uncertainty, however. Whereas in days gone by we assumed that we were contending principally with heredity, now we find we are dealing with the home environment. In days gone by the eldest son might be described as a "chip off the old block." If the old block was a drunkard, let's say a reformed and sober drunkard, he would be grieved to see his son falling into the same trap he himself had fallen into. He would be hurt to realize that his own nature had been passed on to his son. But he would not feel a horrible and futile sense of guilt about his failure to bring the boy up right. Chances are he would comfort himself by saying he had given the boy every warning, every help.

In contrast many modern parents (whatever they may protest to the contrary) feel that it's all their fault. Deeply religious parents are in just as difficult a position as those with no strong religious convictions. "Bring up a child in the way he should go," the Bible says, "and when he is old he will not depart from it." If your child does go wrong then, whose fault can it be but yours, the parents'? As dreaded symptoms appear, they redouble their efforts to follow whatever theory they trust the most.

Am I saying that tradition is right and science wrong? Not at all. I am passing no judgment on either. Rather I am drawing attention to the dilemma we parents find ourselves in.

Underlying our dilemma is a superficial form of determinism, the idea that every effect is the inevitable result of certain causes. The determinism of many child-rearing theories assumes that children are the products of their upbringing. They come into the world as tabulae rasae—clean slates for the parents to write on. If they write what they ought to write (that is, if they rear their children properly), they will produce well-adjusted, outgoing, morally upright and self-reliant children. Any defects in the final product reflect parental mismanagement.

Some parents may be immune to the anxieties of deterministic theories. But many are ridden with guilt and experience times of intense misery. It is bad enough for your children to go wrong. But to know you are responsible for the wrong and to struggle guiltily and unsuccessfully to mend that wrong is a form of torment to which parents of bygone days were less prone than we.

Science, whether its answers are true or false, has made us worse parents than our forefathers. Victorian parents may have been harsh and punitive, but at least they were secure in the knowledge of their virtue. And children need the feeling that their parents (however punitive) know what they are doing. Sailors who serve under a competent skipper who rules his ship as a dictator may grumble at the discipline, but they feel more secure than their mates on a sloppily run ship—and the more so when storms arise.

I believe that the bewilderment, the uncertainty and the lack of confidence of modern parents are more damaging to children than Victorian punitiveness. Children need confident parents. The net result of a deluge of child-rearing articles both religious and secular has been to create two generations of parents who have been anxious, guilty and uncertain of themselves.

In days gone by parents could also blame (sometimes with a certain justice) the influence of "evil companions." Modern parents, with about the same degree of justice, do the same. But social workers, psychologists and psychiatrists are usually quick to point out that the blame lies not with evil companions so much as with inadequate parents. Children may spend six or eight hours a day exposed to ideas and influences alien to the home, but these hours are discounted.

It would be foolish to dismiss everything the behavioral sciences tell us, and such is not my purpose. They can give us facts and statistics which often help us understand behavior. It is interesting to note, for instance, that while juvenile delinquency is far lower in Japan (where tradition assigns more authority to parents) than in the West, the rates of suicide and neurotic illness are higher.

But where are parents to find reliable instructions on child rearing? Perhaps we are asking the wrong question. Perhaps our question should not be, "How can I rear my children successfully?" but, "How can I become a good parent?" For though the two questions appear to be the same, they are in fact different. The first question is concerned with results. It enquires about success, and by success it wants to be assured that the process of child rearing will produce a certain kind of child. The second question leaves the matter of results open. The first question focuses on what parents can *do,* the second on who we should *be.*

When I ask, "How can I become a good parent?" I am asking several other questions such as, "How can I cope with the pains of parenting? What can I do about my personal weaknesses, my impatience, my selfishness, my immaturity, my resentment, my weariness and my doubts? How do I cope with conflict with my spouse?" For I break child-rearing rules in spite of knowing their importance. My problem is less one of ignorance than one of incompetence. What steps can I take to remedy my most glaring defects? One of the main purposes of this book is to respond to that very question.

2
Whose Fault?

Where did I go wrong? Am I still doing things wrong? Am I to blame? Such questions haunt many a parent.

These are crippling questions. They can make you tremble inwardly with anxiety and self-doubt. Instead of setting you free, they impede your footsteps on an icy sludge of uncertainty, rendering you ineffective and indecisive. You become a pathetic victim of fears—fears of doing the wrong thing, fears of the future, fears of more problems, more pain.

Some people would point out that the questions are valueless. What's done is *done.* Water under the bridge. Whether you are wrong or right, regrets serve no purpose. So why worry about past failures?

Their arguments are logical, but self-blame can refuse to take flight in the face of logic. Christians may tell us there is forgiveness for the wrongs we may have done. But often the problem lies in the fact that we aren't altogether clear what we did do wrong. So the questions continue to infest our wakeful nights or to frighten us when a telephone rings. And the nightmare goes on.

It is a futile nightmare. Nothing is achieved by it. When you are in its grip, you not only suffer yourself but cause others to suffer as well. You become less supportive as a husband or wife. Instead of being a pillar in the family, you crumble. You crumble not only from an inner sense of uncertainty and futility but because the very foundations on which you have based your life seem to be giving way.

But you cannot afford to crumble—for your own sake and for your family's. Crumbling will neither undo the past nor help your troubled child. What you need are sure foundations. You need to examine the ground you stand on. Let's look at it together to see if it will bear your weight. If not, let's find ground that will. And when we have found it you will have to learn how to stand firm and strong. You will have to know what resources are available to you and how to use them.

But let's begin at the beginning. Did you go wrong? Certainly you have made mistakes. Every parent has. But are you to blame *for what has happened?* Is it all your fault?

It could be. But it is doubtful that *all* the blame rests on you. Unhappily, as we have already seen, the questions which look so simple are in fact complex. We may consult whatever authority we care to and the unhappy fact remains. Yet consult we must if it is answers we seek. To what authorities should we then look?

I propose to look at three: common sense, science and the Bible. Each has something to suggest, though my personal bias (surprising, perhaps, in a psychiatrist) is to rely mostly on the Bible. Nevertheless all three keep offering us their suggestions, common sense and science a little more pushily than the Bible. Let us turn to them first, reserving a discussion of the Bible for the next chapter.

What Common Sense Says
Why do children turn out as they do? A moment's thought should be enough to tell us that the question is not simply,

Whom do we blame—parent or child?

I have known several families during my life where the parents were a disaster—quarreling, drinking, neglecting the children, running around, partying, separating, divorcing, whatever. Yet their children turned out well. That is to say, they did well at school, got jobs, seemed to have decent friends and now appear to have stable marriages in which they handle their own children sensibly. If you talk to the children, as I have done, they all say, "I swore that *my* home would never be like my parents' home," or, "I saw what booze did in my family, and I swore I'd never touch it," or, "I was the oldest. I knew what it was like to have to look after my kid brothers and sisters night after night. *My* kids are never going to suffer that way."

I am also acquainted with families in which the parents are warm, firm, wise, yet giving—and who have at least one child in serious trouble. Some of the parents are nonreligious, others religious, including sincere Jews, Catholics and Protestants.

On the other hand we have also seen that parenting does make a difference. I checked recently on ten children in serious trouble in our area (this isn't science we're dealing with now but common sense) to find that nine of the ten came from broken homes and all ten from homes where parenting was shocking by any standards.

In other words there are general rules. Good parents are less likely to produce problem children than bad parents. Stable homes are more likely to produce stable children than unstable homes. But that's as far as it seems to go. There are no steel-reinforced rules which say:

Good parenting always produces good children.

Bad parenting always produces bad children.

It simply isn't true. I know that I am not defining my terms carefully. I am looking at *obviously* bad homes and *obviously* problem children—homes and children that most people would without a moment's thought label "bad" and "problem." Defining our terms more carefully would be the gateway to a more scientific approach which I will consider in a moment.

I have a feeling, however, that when doubts and anxieties assail us, common sense is the first thing to go. We long for easy answers, unambiguous assurance. The doubts and guilts drown our minds and make us not *want* to think rationally but instead to cling to any bit of ideological driftwood that comes along. The last thing we want to do when we are drowning is to think logically.

Yet think we must.

As a recently graduated doctor I was given major duties in surgery too early. Within a year of completing my medical training I was frequently responsible at night for all the emergency surgery in a large city hospital as well as in a smaller hospital on one of Britain's major highways. During the day I was often given my own operating list. In less than a year after that I was doing gastrectomies.

Understandably, things sometimes went wrong—seriously wrong. In the operating room a wave of panic would occasionally begin to rise in me as with horror I would see that the operation was getting into a deeper and deeper mess. An unconscious patient's life depended on me. The anesthetist was competent in his or her own area but could offer me no help. Senior surgeons were an hour away. With the panic came a sort of freezing in my brain. My movements were hurried but pointless and repetitive. I would stare at the circle of the eyes of the assisting team, but all eyes would be looking silently back at me.

Under such circumstances the only thing I could do was forcefully to will myself to think slowly and deliberately. I discovered that being a Christian I had been sending up panicky prayers, "Oh, Lord, help! Lord, don't let it go wrong! Lord, don't let me get into a mess! Don't let her die!" They were muttered incantations, not prayer. I had not been aiming at communicating with God but was simply expressing panic in parrot talk.

God of course was merciful. *He* was there. But I saw that *I* had to stop and think. On a spiritual level I had to talk to myself rather than to God. "God *is* here. He doesn't need to be badgered. He *does* care. Now take it easy. What's my *immediate* aim? What should I do first?"

Slowly, as I did this, a mental clearing came. My mind unfroze and I found myself, if not relaxed, at least able to be deliberate and calm. Slowly, with a sense of growing confidence and relief, I found my way through the difficulties, successfully completing what could have been a tragically botched operation. My mind had been freed to accept new ideas, to remember old principles and to force myself to rely on them and go ahead.

I have no doubt that God's Holy Spirit was behind it all. But what was demanded of me in each little crisis was to force myself to stop the panic spiral and think.

I don't know where you may be as you read these words, a parent fearing the future, a parent relaxing a little after the crisis or one in the midst of one. But in our association together, you as reader and I as writer, I must insist on this ground rule: that at times you *force yourself to think* even when you may not feel like it.

Which brings us back to where we started—common sense. Whether you are a Christian or not, you will need plenty of it in dealing with yourself, your family and the child who causes you so much pain. And I say again that common sense says that all the blame does not necessarily lie with you if one of your children goes badly wrong. It may. But it's rarely so simple.

What Science Says
The same turns out to be the case when we turn to science.

Obviously we cannot in a few words cover psychology, sociology, anthropology, ethology, genetics, systems theory, epidemiology, neurophysiology and biochemistry, all of which are among the branches of science that are concerned with the question, Why do people turn out the way they do? Fortunately all we need to do is to note one or two obvious things.

As we look, not at one branch, but at several branches of science, we discover that they are not greatly in conflict with one another so much as preoccupied with different areas of the same subject. The findings of the main branches of the human sciences, for example, anthropology and psychology, are more frequently complementary than they are contradictory.

Anthropology looks at the influence of the culture in which children are reared and notes the correlations between tribal customs and beliefs and the particular characteristics adults display. Margaret Mead, for instance, describes two tribes in one area and their different characteristics. One tribe was hostile and aggressive, another very peaceful and gentle. Mead attributes the differences to child-rearing practices in the two tribes.[1]

But as anthropology has continued to develop it has looked at areas other than child rearing. Different cultures produce different kinds of people. Our own nonscientific views on minority groups may be prejudiced. Or we may think in terms of caricatures. But at least we are right in seeing that there are differences between people of different cultures and that culture appears to have a powerful effect in molding those differences.

If we turn to the psychologies, of which in the West the two most influential seem to be the various learning theories (behaviorism) and psychoanalysis, we find that they take a close-up of why people turn out the way they do. The different schools of psychoanalysis are concerned with what goes on inside growing children in response to their relationships with parents, brothers and sisters, and "significant others" impinging on their development up to adulthood. It is less important for us to be concerned with the particular mechanisms described than with the fact that personality development is studied in terms of the relationships.

Learning theorists are primarily concerned with the way our central nervous system responds to its environment. If I shiver and happen to sit on a warm radiator, I am comforted. My "sitting-on-radiator" behavior is "rewarded" by the pleasure of a warm bottom. The "reward," especially if it is repeated the next time I sit on a radiator, will program me to sit on radiators whenever I shiver in their vicinity.

I have a slight bias toward the various learning theorists in that their views have generally been supported by more careful research and more thorough documentation. But my bias is unimportant. What is important is that behaviorists theorize about the mechanics of how children and their immediate environment interact to affect their behavior and what we might call their personalities.

The area of study is very similar in both schools. Though there are fundamental theoretical differences between the two, both have marshaled evidence in an attempt to show that what happens to children as they grow determines how they will turn out in the end. Moreover, both offer some hope of change for the better where things have gone wrong.

Unhappily the claims they make to help people may be exaggerated. No school of psychology can help someone who refuses help. And this is precisely the problem you may face when your child has gone badly wrong. Leroy might simply refuse all help because he does not want to change or because he fears being labeled abnormal or crazy.

But you will notice that the sciences I have mentioned so far look at two distinct areas. Anthropology, along with sociology, look at the cultural or social setting a child is brought up in.

The psychologies look at the child, and his or her reactions to his or her more immediate environment.

In a way their findings confirm what I indicated in the previous chapter. No single factor can be the sole one (or perhaps even the most significant one) in a child's development. Anthropologists and sociologists merely confirm what we have already seen: the powerful influence of rapid social change, of mass communication and peer-group pressure on growing children. Unlike primitive tribes where family and culture are homogeneous, interwoven into a harmonious system, in our case clashing cultural influences often compete with the home. We are fools to ignore their power.

Branches of science like genetics and to a certain extent epidemiology have a bearing on what characteristics a child can inherit. "Just like his mom," we sometimes say, or, "A chip off the old block."

Nature or Nurture
There was a time when people who believed in heredity and people who believed in environment quarreled fiercely about which of the two was responsible for Sue's piano-playing talent. "She had proper training from an early age, and she idealized her dad [a concert pianist]," one person might say. Such an explanation attributed Sue's flair to environment, the home environment that shaped her early years. Others will say, "It's in the family. They've been musical for generations. It's in their blood." In so saying, they declare themselves on the side of heredity.

In science this became known as the nature/nurture controversy. Some workers argued dogmatically that events from birth on are what matter. Others said that the genes which children inherit from both parents interact to produce not only their physical but their emotional make-up as well as their intelligence.

It is fairly easy to see the importance of genetics in molding *physical* characteristics. Joan doesn't have blue eyes because she admires her mother's blue eyes. She inherited them. It is when we get to less tangible things like predisposition to emotional breakdown, intelligence and character formation that the problem becomes more difficult to sort out.

Epidemiologists tackle the nature/nurture problem in relation to public health. But included in public health are some of the questions I spoke of above. Are emotional breakdowns purely a matter of upbringing and stress? Are some people by nature more vulnerable to them than others? Is there such a thing as an inborn predisposition to crime? Or to alcoholism?

The methods of epidemiologists and geneticists grow more careful and more sophisticated as years go by. Twin studies, for instance, are far more exacting than they were fifty years ago. Do identical twins have more character traits in common than nonidentical twins or than ordinary brothers and sisters? Does it make any difference whether the twins were brought up together or in different families? What happens to children of emotionally disturbed parents or of criminal parents when they are brought up in other homes from infancy? What part do intrauterine events play? Such questions have been tested in increasingly complex surveys.

Few scientists today quarrel about nature versus nurture. Some of us may have a tendency to attach more importance to one than to the other, but most of us agree that both play their part. We speak of "genetic loading" regarding mental breakdowns, illnesses such as schizophrenia and some forms of depression. We recognize that some people have more of an inborn tendency to these things than do others.

What is interesting is to survey some of the more recent work on problems like excessive drinking. Until 1974 few people had any doubt that alcoholism was essentially a product of the way one was brought up and of the way in which one was exposed to alcohol. Theories might differ, but all tended to place the emphasis on nurture rather than nature, on parental example, training and culture rather than on parental genes.

A careful Danish-American study has shown that the old emphasis rests on insecure foundations. D. W. Goodwin and a team of U.S. and Danish workers carried out a careful survey on the children of alcoholic parents. There were two aspects to their study.

First, they took a sizable group of children of alcoholic parents who had been adopted in infancy into nonalcoholic homes and investigated their development into adulthood. Second, they compared the group with a similar group of children, also adopted, but whose natural parents had not been alcoholic.

If environment (parental influence and example and the like) was the main factor in deciding a child's future drinking habits, you would expect that the two groups, both reared in similar adoptive homes, would have produced a similar number of alcoholics. The fact was that the group of men and women whose natural parents were alcoholic produced more than four times the number of alcoholics than the second group, even though both groups had had a comparable upbringing.

Goodwin and his coworkers went on to make a second comparison. Those men and women who had been protected from an alcoholic environment from infancy on were compared with their natural brothers and sisters who had been reared in their own alcoholic homes. *There was no significant difference in the number of alcoholics in the two groups.* The nonalcoholic environment seemed to have afforded no protection for the children of alcoholics adopted in infancy out of alcoholic homes.[2]

What conclusions can we draw from a survey of this nature? It would be a mistake to conclude that a child is born an alcoholic and therefore doomed to become one. All we can say is that the children of alcoholics seem by inheritance to be more vulnerable to the affliction than the children of nonalcoholic parents. What we do not know is whether some total abstainers carry the same "alcoholic gene" which would only show up when one or more of their children were adequately exposed to drink.

But the study is sufficient to make us more aware than ever that genes may not merely be the conveyers of brown eyes, straight teeth and wavy black hair, but of subtle character traits. Our children are shaped not only by the atmosphere in our homes but by the combination of sperm and ovum that united to give them their physical, mental and emotional potential. And as parents we had no control either of the genes we passed on nor of how they interacted when conception took place. Events occurred in the silence of the womb which had a profound bearing on all that was to follow.

It Ain't That Simple
Up to now the main thrust of my argument could be summarized as follows: It ain't that simple. There are too many factors involved for us to be able to assess each one accurately. But I raised a more serious problem earlier. Even if we did know every factor that made a child what he or she now is, would we be any nearer to real understanding?

We have been looking at the law of cause and effect. I have been arguing as though *if we knew enough* (which we don't) we could come up with some sort of formula. We could say John is the way he is because 33.7% of the factors have to do with parenting, 22.4% with general cultural influences, 21.0% with genetic mechanisms of various types and 22.9% with other factors.

But what about John? Did he have no real say? Did he merely *feel* as though he were making choices? Is John nothing more than the sum of the influences that were brought to bear on him? Or is he something more? Is he a person who has made real choices? As a Christian I believe we can never "explain" John scientifically. John is John. He has a will. He chooses. He is pursuing a path he himself selected.

True, there will be times when he will say, "I didn't mean to do it. I tried not to but I couldn't help it!" In so saying he lets us know that his freedom is restricted. At some points he can make choices. At others he finds himself to be a helpless victim of his own weaknesses.

Neither we nor our children are entirely free. Yet neither are we helpless slaves. At times we may groan with St. Paul, "Wretched man that I am! Who will deliver me from this body of death?" (Rom. 7:24). At others we will realize what William Ernest Henley was trying to say when he wrote, "I am the master of my fate; I am the captain of my soul."

We began the chapter with the problem of blame and guilt. We have seen that careful thinking tells us that we can neither take all the credit for our children when they turn out well nor all the blame when they turn out badly. Genes, home environment, school and social environment, and the child's capacity to make certain choices all bear on the final outcome.

Yet a crushing sense of failure haunts many of us. I vividly recall the birth of my oldest boy. As the obstetrician lifted him up by one of his legs my wife cried, "John! His feet! Look at his feet. There's something wrong with them!" Both feet were cruelly clubbed and distorted. There was no skin covering parts of the twisted ankles.

I gazed at the child and said, "They're O.K., honey. There's nothing wrong. They're just fine!" I was not fooling her. Blind to the tragedy, I was emotionally incapable of seeing what was under my nose.

"It's my fault," Lorrie went on with a cry of pain. "It's all my fault! I've given you a crippled baby!"

Each of us displayed common parental defects in that dramatic moment. My weakness was to see only what I wanted to see in my new child and to shut out what I didn't want to see.

Lorrie's was to cry with guilt, a guilt which was as unrealistic as my blindness. All the logical reasoning in the world could have brought her no comfort just then.

The crisis had shown up our parental weaknesses at the very outset of our career as parents. It was a rude beginning to a life of joy, pain, love and grief. For in the whole process we grew, along with the children God gave us. We were not young scientists about to train laboratory rats. We were ordinary parents, beginning a home with a new baby who was soon to demonstrate that he had a mind of his own.

3

False Comfort

*N*ancy was a Christian worker we knew who developed breast cancer when she was pregnant with her second baby. The baby survived. Surgeons removed Nancy's breast and radiologists treated her. The surgeons told her that her chances of living long were poor since the cancer had developed at a time when her breast tissue was at the height of its activity—preparing to secrete milk.

Nancy prayed. Her husband Jon prayed. Lots of us (we were part of the same team) prayed. People in churches prayed. Some prayed for healing, others for grace to accept whatever God might send.

The story is too long to tell in detail. Over a year passed before Nancy eventually died, and during that year she, Jon and several other people were convinced on the basis of the Bible and the Holy Spirit's assurance that God had granted Nancy supernatural healing. Those of us who were unconvinced, were careful not to pour cold water on their convictions though in a letter to Jon I remember suggesting to him that whether Nancy got better or not, we knew that God would be acting in faithfulness and mercy.

There could be no doubt of Jon and Nancy's faith. Certain passages of the Bible seemed to come to them with special force. Nancy was happy, rejoicing in the wonder of God's goodness. She seemed oblivious to her slow, erratic downward course as flesh dropped from her bones and her skin hung loosely on her. Even her deep pain was dismissed as arising from other causes. Jon assured me God had told him, suddenly as he one day knelt in the barn to pray, that he need have no fear. The healing was complete.

I could furnish you with more examples of misplaced faith. But Jon and Nancy stand out in my mind because I loved them —so much so that after two decades the episode still bothers me. Had I been sure they were wrong I could have gone and told them so. But I wasn't sure. In any case wouldn't I have been wrong to snatch away their last twelve months of hope, praise and joy even though they were based on a series of delusions?

It all depends on how you look at it. I've never had a chance to talk the matter over with Jon for we were thousands of miles apart when Nancy died. So I don't know what (apart from grief and loss) he went through. Was his faith shaken for a while? And how about his children, at least the older one who was in on the "healing"? How will his faith about God's direction, about healing, about answers to prayer be affected?

For some people I have known, dashed hope based on a mistaken faith has had more traumatic consequences than unlooked-for bereavement. Their relationship with God has been shaken. If you have been mistaken in trusting God for healing, how do you know that you are not mistaken in a lot of other areas?

A good shake-up can startle us into seeing truth. But something worse than a shake-up has happened to other people. I have watched men and women go on hiding from reality after the initial shock by inventing ever more fantastic insights until they have created another world, a world that appears to me, an observer from outside, to be based on an imaginary relationship with a God of their own making.

Many parents get hurt because they find false hope in the Bible. I do not mean that the Bible is unreliable but that in their concern for their children, parents may read the Bible through magic spectacles. Parents are not alone in this tendency. All of us in trouble are inclined to do the same.

If you are a parent grieving over a child who has gone wrong, you may have to abandon false faith as a first step to finding real faith. You may have been reading into the Bible things that are not there. In this chapter I may begin to tear false hope (based on misunderstood Scripture) from you. It gives me no pleasure to do so. Yet the only hope worth having is hope that is based on truth, and so far as I am capable of giving it, I will give you nothing but what I believe to be solid.

Needless to say it will be for you to decide where the solid ground lies. I am as apt to err as the next person. Yet having known during the forty-five years of my conscious walk with God the terrible pain of mistaking his true voice, his true leading, to follow a series of delusions, I am peculiarly sensitive about the issue of false hope. I bear the scars of scraped knees and have one or two ill-set bones to remind me of past falls. My hair stands on end when I think of the near suffocations I have lived through before a strong hand pulled me from the swamp. Yet I would not be without my scars, my misshaped limbs, my dark memories. They have taught me how *not* to follow my Master.

Promises and Promises

While parents who have no religious beliefs may turn to social workers, psychiatrists, counselors, psychologists, child-development specialists to find answers, Orthodox Jews might consult a rabbi, Roman Catholics a priest, Protestants a minister. In each case the Bible (whether the Torah or the Old and New Testaments combined) might also be looked to as a source both of wisdom and of strength.

Many Protestants along with Orthodox Jews count on certain promises in the Bible. The most quoted one is in the book of Proverbs. "Instruct a child in the way he should go, and when he grows old he will not leave it" (Prov. 22:6 JB). The words are taken as a promise made by God to any parent who rears his or her child in God's ways. Such a child will continue to walk in those ways as he grows older. And since God never welshes on his promises it follows that parents of an erring child may do one of two things. On the one hand they may say, "We brought our daughter up well. Therefore, although things seem very black at the moment, we may count on the promise of God. Sooner or later our girl will return to what she was taught so well when she was a child." In this way they may derive comfort from the promise. On the other hand they may see her delinquency as evidence that they failed as parents, in which case the promise becomes an accusation.

In the diary of a godly missionary mother I read these words (which she gave me permission to quote): "We've given so much thought and prayer to this matter of child rearing; we are open and understanding; we can expect God to honor us by not allowing our children to rebel." Yet one of her children was going sadly astray as I read the words in her diary. God had not "honored" her in the way she expected. Yet in the hours I spent with her and her husband I could not question the soundness and the godliness of the training they had given the child.

Another missionary mother wrote me this: "When this [problem with the child] happens in the home of people that are missionaries in a mission organization, the whole problem is magnified. There is the searching for answers. Someone has failed and it boils down to ... the parents.... The parents have failed to produce a dedicated Christian and the way to prove you are not a failure is to shape that child up and see to it that he has a spiritual experience—and it has to be soon." In her case the same verse from Proverbs was used by fellow missionaries to "prove" parental failure.

A prime rule you must follow in interpreting the Bible is to take into account the context in which you find a given sentence. What about Proverbs 22:6? If you examine its context you will discover that the verse is not a promise made by God to anybody. It is a statement, a *general* statement about how family relationships normally work.

The book of Proverbs is part of what is known as the "wisdom tradition" in Hebrew thought. Unlike the prophetic tradition in which God's messages (of comfort, denunciation and of specific future predictions) are proclaimed to God's people by his prophets, the wisdom literature consists of inspired observations and reflections on daily living by wise and godly men. The sentence "Instruct a child in the way he should go, and when he grows old he will not leave it" is such an observation. It tells us what we can see all around us if only we open our eyes. Good parents usually produce good children.

"Aha," people say to me. "But you're adding a word. You're saying 'usually' and the verse doesn't say that!" True. Neither does it say "invariably." It's not that sort of verse. When we interpret it as an inflexible law, we are reading into it something the Holy Spirit never intended.

Why am I so sure of this? Because the book as a whole makes no sense otherwise. It is a book which presents both sides of the coin: good parenting promotes godliness; disobedient sons are heading for tragedy. It points to examples we can see anywhere, in any culture, in any age. They include observations about disobedient children as well as of good and bad parents. They are divinely inspired observations. It is not their spiritual source that I am calling into question, only the proper way of understanding them.

True, the book contains godly advice about child rearing. Parents are warned that "folly is bound up in the heart of a child, but the rod of discipline drives it far from him" (Prov.

22:15). It has a position on physical discipline that would not meet with modern, scientific approval. "He who spares the rod hates his son, but he who loves him is diligent to discipline him" (Prov. 13:24). As Derek Kidner puts it, "If wisdom is life itself, a hard way to it is better than a soft way to death."[1]

But for the moment we may lay the corporal punishment issue on one side. The point I am making concerns how we should interpret this collection of wise sayings on any issue. And as Kidner points out, the book of Proverbs contains many reminders that "even the best training cannot instil wisdom, but only encourage the choice to seek it."[2]

Read the first four verses of the second chapter. Sons come in at least two varieties. The one will benefit from and welcome discipline, whereas the other will close his ears to it. "A wise man sees the reason for his father's correction; an arrogant man will not listen to rebuke" (Prov. 13:1 NEB). "He who loves wisdom makes his father glad, but one who keeps company with harlots squanders his substance" (Prov. 29:3).

I have never counted the number of verses about bad and good sons or stacked them up against the number of verses about bad or good parents, but the book deals with both. As we look at it as a whole we begin to see why "Instruct a child in the way he should go . . . " is not meant to be an inflexible law. Parents are admonished to bring up children properly. Children are admonished to respond wisely to parental correction. If both play their part all will be well. But it takes a parent-child team working in harmony to produce this happy result. Good parenting is part, perhaps the major part of the story; but a great deal of emphasis is placed on attentive, obedient children who listen and welcome the correction of their parents.

We need not have bothered to consult common sense or science. The ancient wisdom described the facts long ago. God created a world in which Adam himself could choose the folly of disobedience; it must surely follow that the godliest and wisest parents can never guarantee wisdom or godliness in their children. God has given no promise that they ever will be able to. As one parent put it without any bitterness, "You are not just trying to raise your child. You have had to take a piece of damaged goods and are trying to restore it. Sometimes this is much harder."

Misplaced Prayer

There are other wrongly used promises, nonetheless, promises not having to do with rearing children but concerning the nature of prayer itself. "He who has faith in me will do what I am doing; and he will do greater things still because I am going to the Father. Indeed anything you ask in my name I will do," Jesus told his disciples before he left them (Jn. 14:12-13 NEB). "Have faith in God," he said on another occasion. "Truly, I say to you, whoever says to this mountain, 'Be taken up and cast into the sea,' and does not doubt in his heart, but believes that what he says will come to pass, it will be done for him. Therefore I tell you, whatever you ask in prayer, believe that you have received it, and it will be yours" (Mk. 11:22-24).

What better assurance could a grieving parent have of God's intervention? Where could you find more all-embracing promises than in such words? Few things are more needed in the church today than Christians prepared to count without question on the power and faithfulness of our God. For the moment I must warn against the misuse of verses I have quoted.

Whenever you pray for something, you must take into account two aspects of your request. You must consider both its difficulties and its nature.

Moving mountains is difficult. Mountains are rarely thrown into the sea. None that I know of has been thus thrown in answer to prayer. But the difficulty of moving mountains is the very point Jesus was thinking of when he used so extreme an example. He was not talking merely of metaphorical mountains but of tons of rock and stone. If God's plans required Mount Everest to be hurled across the globe into the Pacific, you could ask him to do it and in response to your faith he would. There is nothing too hard for God. Shifting Everest is a small matter to a God who flings universes through time. So if the difficulty of our request raises its head, we need have no fear. His power has no limits, his kindness and concern for us, no measure.

However, we must consider the nature as well as the difficulty of the request. Consider the following examples.

"God, will you please kill my next-door neighbor? I hate him. I hereby place my faith in you that you will get him knocked down by a car tomorrow. I do not have the least doubt that you will bring this to pass. In Jesus' name. Amen!"

"God, please enable me to lie and deceive expertly so I can swindle the money I need out of my business partner. I ask it in absolute faith in the name of Jesus. Amen!"

You can see at once that God would not answer such prayers. The reason would not be due to their technical difficulty. "Accidents" cause him no problems. He can close a person's eyes to an approaching car as easily as to an approaching swindler. But such blasphemous requests do violence to the nature of God and his kingdom. He refuses to be the instrument of murderous hate or theft. He refuses in fact to be the instrument of anything or anyone.

You will tell me doubtless that you would not dream of making the kind of request I used in my examples. No matter. The examples may be extreme, but you can see the point. There are certain things God *will not* do, however great our faith may be. When we pray, therefore, we must ask ourselves, "Am I requesting things that are consistent with God's nature, his designs, his kingdom, his will?" For prayer was not designed primarily for our comfort (though it can provide us with great comfort) but to enable us to collaborate with Christ in bringing about his kingdom. The context of the words of Jesus that I quoted in both instances makes this much clearer. And I must continue to insist that it never seems to be God's will to force his blessings down anyone's throat.

"We have learned a lot in the past few years that we never would have [learned] without the problems," writes a missionary mother of four daughters, two of whom brought disgrace and shame on her. Her letter to me continued, "I have come to a few conclusions that I will share with you. First, I believe that God gave each of us a free will that we use. The problem arises when we find out that our children have one and are using it."

God may go to great lengths. C. S. Lewis once stated that he was brought into the kingdom of God "kicking, struggling, resentful, and darting [my] eyes in every direction for a chance of escape."[3] But even Lewis makes it clear in much of his writing that this phrasing is not to be taken too literally. In fact it was his intellect, rather than his will, which was dragged, kicking and screaming to face the truth. God, in love, will go to any length to bring a man or woman to face reality. Paul was subjected to a terrible light and to physical blindness. But God will not (to switch metaphors) force any horse to drink the water he has pulled him to.

Here lies a key to understanding how we may pray for our own children or for anyone else. We may ask with every confidence that God will open the eyes of the morally and spiritually blind. We may ask that the self-deceptions which sinners hide behind may be burned away in the fierce light of truth, that dark caverns may be rent asunder to let the sunlight pour in, that self-disguises may be stripped from a man or woman to reveal the horror of their nakedness in the holy light of God. We may ask above all that the glory of the face of Christ will shine through the spiritual blindness caused by the God of this world (2 Cor. 4:4). All of this we can ask with every assurance that God will not only hear but will delight to answer.

But we may not ask him to *force* a man, woman or child to

love and trust him. To deliver them from overwhelming temptation: yes. To give them every opportunity: yes. To reveal his beauty, his tenderness, his forgiveness: yes. But to force a man against his will to bow the knee: not in this life. And to force a man to trust him: never.

I could go on multiplying instances of wrongly used promises. But my point should be sufficiently clear by now. Nancy and Jon come back into my mind. They remind me of so many Christians I have known who grapple with verses such as I have been quoting in ways that are destructive to their own spirits and painful to their consciences: " . . . and does not doubt in his heart. . . . " How they scrutinize the dark corners of their hearts for concealed and lingering doubts! How torturously they force themselves to achieve subjective feelings of faith! Others have less difficulty. They slide into a world of make-believe, groping from vision to vision among mists of fantasy. They are shielded from pain because they are shielded from reality. Their prayers are addressed to a god of their own creation; their faith has become self-deception.

How to Manipulate God

I said earlier that God refuses to be the instrument of anything or anyone. Yet Christians unconsciously try to use him like that—by the ferocity of their faith, by their attempts to bargain with him. Most tragic of all, recent years have seen Christians try to use praise as a crude instrument to bring God to heel.

Let me explain what I mean. God has used the charismatic movement to remind many of us that we had forgotten how to praise him. The stress on praise, worship and new freedom in worship (by no means now confined to charismatics) owes itself in part to the movement's influence. In this respect its effect on us has been healthy.

God's people *ought* to praise him. He deserves our praise. And amazingly, our own spirits are uplifted and our souls enlarged as in private or as in fellowship together we magnify his name. We discover a new dimension in our lives. We begin to realize why we were created.

But praise has other spin-offs. It can knock your depression for a loop. You may begin to praise from a pit of gloom to rise to regions of light and joy. Nor are the effects temporary. Provided you are not depressively ill, praise as a way of life can transform your daily experience to one of ongoing joy.

Again pietists down the ages (long before the modern charismatic movement began) have preached the virtues of praise as a response to personal trial and tragedy. Do I suffer persecution? Have I encountered personal tragedy? Then let me praise God. I have been selected for a high honor. I must praise him not so much for the tragedy but that I know him to be faithful in it, that the very tragedy might have been allowed to do a deeper work in my spirit, to bring a greater freedom in my service. God is bringing a great good out of something evil.

So far so good. Praise is right and we must praise God more. We can only do so, of course, if we trust him. And in praising him we will (as secondary benefits) discover we are being uplifted, purified, strengthened.

Even in these things, however, there are subtle dangers. Please observe carefully. Praise is not a psychological technique. It must never be pursued for its benefits. It is good to praise God when you feel down, but we must praise him because he is worthy of praise, not because we will get a lift out of doing so. Praise is not the spiritual equivalent of winning the homecoming game.

But the danger, both of blasphemy and of personal psychological destruction, becomes acute when we become fascinated with what has been termed "praise power." Spiritual power can unquestionably be released on earth when God's people exult in his majesty and greatness. There are dramatic biblical and extrabiblical accounts of the phenomenon.

But today it is promoted as a gimmick.

My friend Jean has a seventeen-year-old daughter who drinks too much, has been on and off drugs of various sorts, has made three suicide attempts and had two illegal abortions. Jean is a single parent, torn apart both by the frustration of trying to keep a home together (she has two younger children) and by mingled rage and compassion toward her oldest daughter.

"Try praise power," a Christian friend advised.

"Praise power?"

"Yes. Have you never praised God that Sasha tried to commit suicide? Have you never praised him that she drinks so much?"

Jean was shocked. But desperate, she was ready to clutch at straws. She knew enough of the Bible to be dubious about the theology of the suggestion, but she could not resist the force of her friend's enthusiasm and her glowing accounts of "deliverance through praise power."

"God *has* to respond to praise! He can't resist it! What's more, the devil can't stand it. Demons take flight. Just praise him, Jean! Praise him for the mess she's in! Praise him because you're torn in two and can't stand it anymore! Praise him that he will come in and take over!"

The example I quote is not extreme. People have said similar things to me personally. On a number of counts I damn their advice as God dishonoring and harmful. It may lift my mood but only by a psychological trick.

First, we are not called on to praise God for evil. *He* does not rejoice in it and neither should we. To praise him for it is like praising a mother because her baby has been run over by a car. It is as revolting as it is inappropriate.

Second, praise is an expression of trust and gratitude, not a technique for exerting pressure on God. Not all Christians put it so explicitly as Jean's friend, but there are books that do. I know that in some places the Bible depicts God as "repenting of his evil" in response to human repentance and earnest prayer. But nowhere is praise seen as a weapon placed in the hands of human beings to make God do something human beings want him to. You can't manipulate God with any technique. Praise power, as it is currently taught and practiced, is a form of blasphemy. It reduces God to a celestial vending machine. Insert some praise, select the right button, then get whatever you want.

Understandably, the consequences can be just as tragic for those who practice it as a form of the misplaced faith I spoke of earlier. I can think of few things more heart-rending than a grief-stricken man with a vacant face mouthing praises to God because his son lies dying in a hospital after smashing a car up when he was drunk, mouthing praises since this is the way to raise up his son from a death bed to a life of service for God.

The man's heart is torn apart. His life is in pieces. It would be different if his praise was the praise of a broken man who could say "I don't understand, but I do believe you are faithful. And even in the dark I am going to go on trusting you!" Behold instead a man forcing himself with an iron will to utter incantations of magical "praise," telling us all that because he has praised, God will not fail him.

How cruel the merchants of praise power are! For when the boy dies, what is the father's response? "I guess we just weren't faithful enough in praising God!" Tragedy and death are hard enough to face without our being saddled by the guilt arising from soul-destroying, God-manipulating superstitions.

God cannot be manipulated. But he can occasionally be provoked by such attempts. Once his people "had a wanton craving in the wilderness, and put God to the test in the desert; he gave them what they asked, but sent a wasting disease among them" (Ps. 106:14-15). A wise parent may occasionally do the same, letting a child learn from bitter experience how detestable is the very thing they had thought so desirable. We may know what we want. We might even succeed (if we are foolish enough) in getting what we want. But before we praise God, let us be sure we are in tune with him and that anything we request coincides with what he wants for us and for our children.

Infant Baptism and the New Covenant
The following concerns people who pin their hopes on what may be another misunderstanding of the Scriptures—Bible covenants. Some people are angry with me when I suggest that children (children of godly parents) who are baptized not merely as a rite but as an expression of the parents' trust in God's covenant faithfulness are not immune from spiritual tragedy. As I said in *The Fight*, "The best parents in the world sometimes produce monsters; while the breakers of every child-rearing rule may produce a family of responsible, adjusted little angels. It happens all the time."[4] If you are the kind of Christian parent who is upset by such an assertion and if your disagreement with me arises from your view of God's covenant faithfulness, it may be helpful to look at the areas where we agree as well as those where we disagree.

I shall not discuss the issue of infant baptism itself. Equally sincere Christians may differ about its appropriateness as well as about its precise significance. I leave the issue on one side because it does not lie at the core of the difficulty we are discussing. Many people who practice infant baptism do so with the full recognition that they may be baptizing a future "monster."

God's covenants embody special promises to which God binds himself. Confusion arises because the promises may concern both a person and his or her descendants. For instance, years before God's New Covenant was established, its contents were revealed to Jeremiah: "I will give them one heart and one way, that they may fear me for ever, for their own good and the good of their children after them" (Jer.

32:39). Yet God's covenant promises are conditional. Only those who keep the covenant will enjoy its benefits. It follows that while God's covenanted promises have in mind the well-being of our children, they, like us, are required to meet their covenant obligations if God's purposes are to be fulfilled.

Jeremiah makes it very clear before describing the New Covenant that God's promises do not violate the principle of personal responsibility. "In those days they shall no longer say: 'The fathers have eaten sour grapes, and the children's teeth are set on edge.' But everyone shall die for his own sin; each man who eats sour grapes, his teeth shall be set on edge" (Jer. 31:29-30). Ezekiel expounds the principle in much greater detail, extending the idea that covenant blessings and punishments are meted on the basis of an individual's response to the covenant (Ezek. 18:1-24). Thus while a covenant (just like proverbial counsel) makes provision for benefits and blessings to the child of godly parents, it does not guarantee them. God's covenant to David, fully understood with all its implications for good and ill by his son Solomon, did not in fact secure ongoing safety and prosperity for Israel, for Judah or for every descendant of David. God was faithful. The covenant remained in effect and still does. "If the law that I made for the day and the night could be annulled, . . . then my covenant with my servant David could be annulled so that none of his line should sit upon his throne" (Jer. 33:20-21 NEB). It was first made explicit to David in 2 Samuel 7:8-16 and is also referred to in Psalm 89:19-37 and Psalm 132. "Your family shall be established and your kingdom shall stand for all time in my sight, and your throne shall be established for ever" (2 Sam. 7:16 NEB).

It is easy for us by hindsight to explain or even to explain away these words. Yet put yourself in David's shoes for a moment. Had he taken these words alone and failed to observe the full wording of the covenant, he could have inferred an unbroken ruling line was to extend from him forever. Nothing of the kind took place. In the end God's promise was fulfilled in Christ. But had David extracted from the covenant the parental comfort he personally might have wished to or had he taken it as a mechanical prediction of inevitable, interminable, uninterrupted, prosperous Davidic rule, he would have been clinging to a false hope.

Our desire for parental comfort can, as I said earlier, betray us into reading into Scripture something that is not there. God's covenants may reveal his grace, but our participation in them is meant to serve his glory rather than our personal comfort. God's choice of the house of David was not dictated for David's benefit any more than for the benefit of David's children. Such benefits might or might not accrue to them. Wider plans of mercy and the revelation of God's own glory were behind the covenant.

If only we could get things sewn up, we could rest in peace. If only we could have a guarantee that, come what might, all would be well with our children, we could breathe easily and die content. And who can blame any parent for having such desires? Do not our yearnings spring, at least in part, from the yearning heart of the heavenly Father? But the covenants with Abraham, with Moses, with David and with us are not mechanical affairs. Biblical history, if it teaches us nothing else, should make this much clear.

Let me ask you, you who know God has already given you a new heart and an inner yearning to follow him, Do you always do so? Does your new heart make it impossible for you to fall into sin? If you yourself are not immune from the possibility of rebellion, do you suppose your children can be?

Yet, you ask me, did not Paul assure the Philippian jailer that his faith would mean salvation for his whole household? And was not every member of the jailer's household baptized after due instruction? Yes, indeed (to both questions). But it is a very long leap from the joy of that blessed occasion to an assumption that the jailer's children (if indeed he had any children) grew up as shining trophies of grace. It is not even clear that the salvation about which the jailer initially called out, had to do with sin at all. It is more likely that his fears, and Paul's rejoinder, had to do with physical salvation from the wrath of the civic authorities over escaped prisoners.

There can be no doubt, of course, that a subsequent work of grace was done in the jailer's household. But let us not infer from such slender evidence that God has promised to override our children's powers of choice. Such has never been an aspect of God's covenant faithfulness. It violates his character and his basic relationship with every member of the human race.

"What about Me and Adam?"

A deeper question underlies the problems we have been considering. Several times I have mentioned the philosophical issue of determinism. A determinist believes no one makes any decisions. People may think they do, but it is all an illusion. Freedom, your freedom and mine, to make choices does not in fact exist. On those occasions when we think we are choosing to do something, we are merely acting out a role determined for us by heredity and environment. Given enough data, a good scientist could have predicted our choice before we made it.

Some Christians feel that God's sovereign control over the universe automatically takes away any free choice in the same way determinism does. The Bible does in fact teach that God *chooses* those to whom he will show mercy. "So it depends not upon man's will or exertion, but upon God's mercy" (Rom. 9:16). That is why we speak not merely of God's grace, but of God's *sovereign* grace.

So far I have been arguing strongly that God does not force his mercy down anyone's throat but that everyone may choose to refuse it. I have maintained that God's relationships with human beings from Adam on demonstrates this. Yet Paul's statement in Romans (and others like it) demands that I take a second look at my position.

I have no relish to get into the classic free will/election controversy. In the past it nearly drowned me in swirling whirlpools of angry and powerful words. And if those with greater minds and superior scholarship than mine failed to resolve the issue (which is at base philosophical rather than theological), how can I resolve it in a paragraph or two?

Perhaps it would be better to consider what Paul was arguing about when he made his strong statement in Romans 9:16. In reading the whole of the epistle to the Romans carefully, one sees that his concern is not to raise the issue about whether we have free will, but to emphasize that God is not only all-powerful and sovereign but also merciful and gracious, that no man ever has the right either to complain against him or to boast before him. Did I choose to accept his mercy? Let me not boast but bow in the dust before him! I dare not take the least particle of credit before a God who freely gave me both to understand and to choose his mercy.

Your children can be given an understanding of the things of God however alienated from God they now are or may yet become. They can be given the capacity to see clearly and to choose. It is for these things you may plead. They are your children's covenant rights. But you, as a parent, have neither the right nor the ability to control your child's destiny. It is a matter that will be resolved between your child and God.

I remember a sunny summer day in Paris when I knelt in a beautiful park to pray for a second child. Four years had passed since the birth of our first child, and we were impatient for a larger family. As time passed we consulted clinics, but our apparent infertility had no physiological explanation. My prayer was earnest but routine. It included an oft-repeated clause in my proposed contract with God which ran roughly, "Of course I want the child to be a credit both to me and to you. I would like him or her to be a true disciple of Jesus

Christ. Otherwise, I would rather do without."

A thought exploded like a bomb in my brain. From the cloudless blue the reply seemed to come, "What about me and Adam?"

Instantly I knew what he was saying. God had not made us automata but had created us in his image with wills of our own and therefore with the capacity to choose to please God or to displease him, to obey him or to rebel against him. We chose not God's way but our own.

God must have known in advance what would happen. Past, present and future are all one to him. He must have foreseen the wars, the cruelty, the whole horror of human history. Yet knowing, he still gave us the gift not of mere existence but of life.

The theological problem is enormous and I could not discuss it adequately even if there were time to do so. But with horror I saw not only what God was asking me, but the selfishness and shallowness of the escape clause in my proposed contract.

Was I willing, like God, to give the gift of life whatever the consequences might be, no matter how my child might choose to use that life? A hundred ugly possibilities flashed on the screen of my mind. A growing fear filled me. I was asking God to let me bring life into being. He was telling me I would not have control of what the fruit of my body might do with the life I gave. Was I still willing to give life to someone who might bring me humiliation, pain, disgrace?

The question is basic to an understanding of all human relationships, not only to those of parent and child. We may teach; we may admonish; we may train; we may discipline; we may love. But unless in the case of a child we see him or her as much more than an extension of ourselves, we have not begun to learn what life is all about.

In a moment of terrible despair and grief have you ever wished that one of your children had never been born? Or

57

have you wished that he or she might conveniently die or disappear? How many times have you cried, "I just cannot take any more"? Perhaps your pain and shame may have been made worse by the fact that you had yet to learn the most basic rule of all. You cannot ever control another human being, even if that human being is your own child. You do not have the right to. You may discipline and teach; you may train; you may point the right course; you may "shape behavior patterns"; you may reason; you may plead. But you cannot and may not ever control. God has placed your child's ultimate destiny within your child's own hands.

It was not easy for me to say, "Yes. Give me the power to beget another child . . . whatever course that child may eventually choose in life." But I said it. And I meant it. When I got to my feet I was not the same person as when I knelt down.

The insight I was given on that sunny afternoon in Paris has not shielded me from parental suffering. But it has given me a basic guideline, a rope to hold on to in the dark, a way to grope forward when I could not see ahead. It was my first (but by no means my last) lesson in what being a parent means.

II

Parents
in
Pain

4

Erosion of Trust: The Pain Begins

Martha had written in her diary about her daughter, "Certain disturbing traits find expression from time to time causing a slight ripple on the naturally calm waters. But with firmness and understanding we can control these, and certainly nobody but our most trusted friends know. . . . "

The anxiety had begun. That is to say, it had begun to rise above the level of normal parental anxiety. There was nothing to be alarmed about yet. Or was there? As a matter of fact, though at the time she did not know it, there was. With her permission I read the rest of the diary and knew what was to come. But when Martha wrote the entry she knew nothing for certain. She only knew that a vague premonition of approaching trouble made her ill at ease.

The diary continued. "We heard of a case of a trusted teenager who for a year had been successfully deceiving his parents. But things finally caught up with him and the truth was out: drugs, stealing, etc. And he had understanding Christian parents just like us. PANIC. 'Lord, if this happened to us I'd go crazy. I couldn't take it!' "

It did happen. She didn't go crazy. She *did* "take it." Perhaps a clue to her strength is found in a later letter.

". . . But the seesawing between peace and no peace bothered me. Then there seemed to be a real breakthrough when I was convicted that overanxiety was a sin to be repented of and that spending more time listening to the devil's 'what ifs' than to God's truths was causing the overanxiety. About that time I began studying the Psalms, unhurriedly with the Tyndale Commentary. I was startled and so very comforted by their relevance."

Perhaps Martha had at first wondered whether she was doing what I had done the first time I saw Scott's feet—refusing to see what was there. But who can know? Where is the fine line between troublesome behavior that will sort itself out eventually and the signs of an approaching hurricane?

Some parents I have known worried their children into delinquency. "I know what you've been doing. You've been being a bad girl!" Or, "You're nothing better than a little tramp." And all the time the "little tramp" has been a normal, good girl doing very normal things.

Boys and girls have wept in psychiatrists' offices telling the same story. "They kept on accusing me. They wouldn't stop. It didn't matter what I said; they'd never believe me. So in the end (what the heck?) I figured I might as well do all the things they said I was doing. It made no difference anyway."

There is a difference between healthy parental anxiety and the kind of thing I've just described. Unwarranted suspicion voiced with hostility is unforgivable. Martha's problem was light-years from that.

Finally there may come a major shock. "Then Donna wrote some filthy letters to boys who wrote the same kind of thing back," one mother wrote me. "These letters were found by the staff [of a religious school] and we were told about it."

She never told me whether she herself had a chance to read the letters or not, but I remember the shocked reaction of another mother who did. "I was cleaning her drawers out. Her room gets so messy that at times I just have to go and clean it up. And there were these letters. I guess I shouldn't have read them, but they were lying there open so I did. Photographs too. I couldn't believe it! I sat down in a state of shock for half an hour. Where did she learn all this? And that boy.... They were both children [boy, thirteen; girl, fifteen]. I couldn't understand some of the words, but filthy.... They talked about all the different kinds of sex they'd had, how smart they were getting at shoplifting, what fools parents and police were. Jean never said anything bad about us, but the boy said unbelievable things about his parents. And Jean was boasting (why she never mailed the letter I don't know) about pushing dope and how much money she made, how much she stole, how often she played truant from school, how she planned to run away and live with him...."

She had sat down amid the rumpled bedclothes on her daughter's unmade bed while the universe turned slowly upside-down. Thoughts refused to take shape. Rage of a kind she had never before experienced, a blind and murderous rage that shocked her even more than the letters she had read, left her frightened, breathless, weak. Then through the rage, pain began to make itself felt, a pain with no hint of self-pity in it (she was too angry for self-pity) and a pain she was to feel for two or three years at varying levels of intensity.

Had she known that younger teen-agers tend to exaggerate and top one another's letters, rather like fishermen telling fish stories or comedians trying to cap one joke with a better one, her pain might have been lessened a little. In any case the thoughts such letters reveal may be harbingers of the very behavior they describe.

Barbara Johnson of Melodyland wrote to me about her Spatula Club. "You need a bit of humor. Parents have to be scraped off the ceiling when they first find out. So we make these little spatulas. . . . "

"Scraped off the ceiling." The phrasing is apt. It is so often (for the parents) the way the pain begins. Hitting the ceiling is only the start. It is being scraped down; landing on the hard floor; slowly putting pieces of yourself together again; getting creakingly to your feet and beginning to walk. (There is no choice; you have to go on.) It is in doing all this that the pain begins. And it must all be done without laying the pain and resentment on your family—most especially on the child who has caused your hurt. They know they've hurt you. You need not, you must not grind their faces into the dirt.

Not all parents reach the ceiling. Horror, like a striptease artist, may let herself be seen tantalizingly, a little at a time. For Jeremy it all began when his thirteen-year-old daughter Rhonda was raped (or when she called on the phone from the local police station, crying and saying she had been raped) and when he and his wife Jennifer went down to the police station to be present, as the police gently and kindly probed her story. ("I cannot speak too highly of the police. They were really so gentle, so kind and patient.")

But as months passed, details of Rhonda's story grew more elaborate and more puzzling. Her accounts of subsequent late nights didn't check out. Slowly it became apparent, slowly as one piece of the jigsaw after another began to fit into place, that Rhonda was the willing centerpiece of a high-school sex ring and that the rape story was phony. For Jeremy and Jennifer it was not a matter of one big shock but of an endless series of humiliations and griefs as one little piece of information after another came to light, pieces slowly building a sordid picture. Jeremy told me about the final piece without any expression in his quiet voice. "Apparently it started with incest in our home years ago. My second boy Ralph and Rhonda were. . . . " He looked away. I have no idea what he was thinking, and I didn't ask him.

Facing the Problems

At one point I wondered whether to deal with the different kinds of trouble children get into: drugs, alcohol, crime, homosexuality, secret marriages, pregnancy/paternity and so on. Yet I realized that in one sense it makes little difference what the nature of the problem is. Parental reactions run along the same lines. Shock is shock. Mistrust is mistrust. Rage is rage, weariness is weariness and despair, despair. Whatever the cause of our struggles, our human reactions follow similar patterns. And it is these you need help with. I want to give you a hand in getting up off the floor to live, even to experience joy again.

My goal is higher yet. I would like to open a door for you, a "door of hope in the Valley of Achor" through which you may enter a fuller and richer life than you could have known before. For the God I believe in specializes in bringing good out of evil, strength out of pain and joy out of tragedy.

The goodness begins when you face the truth squarely, however much it sickens you. As much as you want to walk away and live someplace else, you did marry. You did produce children. They are alive and they are yours. The problems won't go away by pretending they are not there.

The problems include your feelings—your hurt, your rage, your panic, your disappointment, your shame, your humiliation, your alternate wish to yell at someone (your spouse, your child, your child's friends, the schoolteacher) and to lock yourself in the bathroom and talk to nobody. Look at them all. They exist. They are part of the problem you face. Even the sense of despair. And to look at them, to be able to face them fully and honestly, and to size them up is the first step in solving them. You cannot solve problems you close your eyes to.

Learning Mistrust

"You just have no idea," you tell me. "I think I could take anything, *anything,* if only I could trust him. It's this lying, lying,

lying—this endless stealing that I can't take. How much longer must we go through the same hassles over and over again?"

A woman I know wrote me some notes on her reactions. "With the first definite act of defiance covered up by deceit, I was shattered. After all, we could explain why he did it, we could see why it wasn't easy for him to accept the rules we laid down, but he actually deliberately defied us and coldly planned how to cover it up. Deep hurt. How could he do this to us, betray our trust and brush aside our obvious concern to do what we were sure was best?

"I was forced to the shattering realization that we were not progressing and that it was not working out as the books led us to believe. ('Establish and maintain a good relationship with your children. Be firm and loving and your child will feel secure.') . . .

"Then I imagine: what does he do, anyway, when he's out with his friends? Was he *really* late for the reasonable reason he gave? Did he bring back the correct change? Did he go where he said he was going or somewhere else we would not approve of? Was I right to have always assured him I'd never accuse him of anything unless I had certain proof? Was I right to have asked his forgiveness on several occasions when I did [accuse] and he denied it? *Yes.* I've always felt this was right."

Yet, soul of honesty, sensitivity and integrity that she was, she was being naive and was paying dearly for her naiveté.

"I had to learn to *love Jane without trusting her,*" one father told me slowly. "Evil affected the relationship between us, and we had to recognize it openly. To love doesn't mean to close one's eyes to something."

Months later Jane was to tell her father with despairing tears, "Daddy, I've lied so much I don't know when I'm lying anymore." Years before, varying sums of cash had disappeared from the house over a period of several years, and Jane told her father about it, at least about what she could remember.

"And truth, honesty and so on had been so important to us as a family," her father told me. "We had talked about it and practiced it. But with Jane...."

In many homes bitterness and accusations erupt volcanically.

"You're lying!"

"I'm not lying. I never even *saw* the money. I never went *near* your room."

"John, you can't fool me. I can always tell when you're lying."

"I'm *not lying.*" (John is screaming now, his eyes blazing and his fists clenched.) *"You never believe ME! You don't trust me!"*

"Of course I don't. Why should I? How often have you acted just like you are now, and then in the end you have to own up. What I hate about this whole thing is that you've never *yet* told the truth *until you've had to,* until the proof's so obvious that you can't deny it anymore."

"Well, I'm not lying now."

And so bitterness spreads, destroying the family's peace, corroding each member with acid. For the present nothing is solved. Parent and child are antagonists. The parent is enraged or depressed, less over the loss of money or some valuable (a camera, a bottle of sleeping pills or of whiskey) than over the stalemate, the inability to penetrate the child's defenses, to prove the wrongdoing. The child, on the other hand, is besieged with hostility.

To most parents it is the weariness, the ongoing atmosphere of mistrust that is hardest to bear. Some parents wake in the night to hear a door opening or closing. A visit to the bathroom? Then the worry. "Did I put away everything that I should have? What did I do with Bert's Christmas present? And my new earrings? Did I leave my car keys in my coat pocket?" (There are so many things to think about in a large family.) Slowly a mother or a father gets out of a warm bed and reaches for a bathrobe in the dark to check the house.

For many it is the anxious moment when they discover that something is missing. Mislaid? Hidden in some special place that's now forgotten? "I have a feeling I put it in a drawer. Or did I?" Then the sickening doubts. The family silently divides itself into those among whom trust exists and those among whom it does not. Occasional bursts of accusatory rage among the children disrupt the calm, and one or both parents sit tensely wondering whether and when to intervene.

"Daddy, I don't *want* to keep stealing," fourteen-year-old Kim protested tearfully. "I don't know why I do it. My social worker says I do it because I'm looking for more love. But I *know* you guys love me. I keep saying I won't do it anymore and then I do. I guess I'm just a lousy thief. I've prayed for victory. I've yielded to the Holy Spirit like the pastor said. And then I steal again. I don't think I'll ever stop. Daddy, how *do* you stop stealing?"

Daddy didn't know. He'd never stolen in his life.

The only thing he could think of right then was to do all he could to make sure not to throw temptation in Kim's way, which meant hiding his wallet every night, keeping his car keys hidden, and locking certain drawers and doors. It also meant letting her know he understood she had a problem without giving her the idea he would go along with her stealing. It meant hard thinking about how Kim could pay back her thefts and yet allow her some spare time, some leisure and fun. And that problem was a tough one. For not only had Kim stolen a great deal, but she had also been a work dodger.

Neither Condoning nor Rejecting

Children lie out of fear of what will happen if they tell the truth. Yet responsible parents can never pretend to their children that bad behavior is going to be ignored in the future. You cannot cure lying by protecting your child from the consequences of wrongdoing. You may, of course, have been too severe, too harsh and rejecting in the way you dealt with past disobedience so that your child has an exaggerated fear. He or she lies out of realistic terror. But even so the damage is done now and the practical problem that faces you is how to reduce the fear. Can it be reduced since you must not say, "O.K., we'll never get mad again, and we'll never punish you whatever you do"? In any case some children whose parents have not been unreasonable in their discipline still lie.

So the difficulty remains. As parents we face the problem of teaching children to do something good and praiseworthy (to tell the truth) when their well-doing will be rewarded with discipline.

What about your feelings? Your child has a problem. She or he lies and steals. You are helpless, utterly so, to stop your child from lying and stealing whenever she or he chooses to. It is unlikely that the lying and stealing will stop overnight. You may both face a long haul.

So accept the fact. Fretting and fuming over it will help neither of you. You won't change anything by getting furious about it, in fact you will only make matters worse.

Face it. Tim has a problem. He lies and steals. But remember at the same time that some part of him wishes he could stop lying and stealing. This may not have occurred to you. You may be inclined to use words like *deliberate* and *willful*. Yet Tim's defiance could be nothing more than a cover for his helplessness and guilt. True, he does lie deliberately—in one sense at least. Is not all sin deliberate? Is there not a point in every temptation when, knowing that something is wrong, we make a choice between the pull of it and the clamor of our weak conscience? Tim's lies are no more "deliberate" (and no less) than your own bitterness over them.

It will help you to see this. It will help you beyond measure to stop viewing the matter as a struggle of wills between the two of you. Unconsciously, you see, you may have been assuming that you had the power to make him tell the truth at all times, to turn him into a truthful son by the force of your

determination, the exercise of your patience, the distress of
your tears, the logic of your arguments. But you will never do
it once the habit is well established. And the struggle to do so
may destroy both of you. The problem is one which only God
and Tim can solve.

Lying and stealing have become "besetting sins" for him.
They have become habits, habits he is powerless to break, and
you must see them in this way, see him as weak in the face of
temptation. Search your own life for a particular weakness
you have little or no power over. Now try to remember that
your child has as little power over lying and stealing as you
have over your own problem.

Tim is vulnerable to temptation. Before every lie is invented, there has been a temptation to lie. The temptation
may occur long before the lie is uttered. And at an earlier
stage in his experience there may have been a struggle before
he decided to deceive you. It may be that now he has learned
to brush temptation aside quickly, to put on a superb act. But
the temptation was there and is still. And when he begins the
long uphill course of learning to be truthful again, he will face
not lessening temptation but *increasing* temptation. As his
conscience is progressively reawakened to do battle with the
lying mental habits he now slips into so readily, he will need all
the help and sympathy he can get in his struggle against sin.

Therefore you must establish a new attitude in yourself and
a new understanding with your child, the kind of understanding I hinted at earlier. The problem is your child's, not yours.
You cannot solve his problem for him, so quit trying. Until he
wants with all his heart to deal with it, until he himself cries out
for help—to Christ, to you—nothing will ever take place.
Until that time all you can do is pray and adjust your life to the
problem, making what changes you can to protect yourself,
your child and the rest of the family from his untrustworthi-
ness.

Yet you should not assume that he likes lying or that his conscience is satisfied with it. Whatever his outward attitude may be, however defiant his statements are, he has an inner hunger for truth God placed there, a hunger that will never die and that nothing but truth can satisfy. It is important that you let him know that. It is important that you make yourself his ally, the ally with the deepest desires and longings.

But it is also important that you face the real issues of deception. Some books tell you that children respond to trust. Trust them and they will begin to earn more of your confidence. Be suspicious of them and they will learn to lie and deceive.

I suppose there is a measure of truth in the idea. Of course children like to be trusted. Don't we all? But this is not the whole story. Some children feel safer with controls. To one child trust will be a joyful door to a deepening relationship, to another a terrible temptation to choose between the relationship and something that is (temporarily) a fierce attraction.

Therefore parent and child must face the issue of lying and deception not once, but many times. It is best if it can be done in an atmosphere of calm. I recognize this is not always easy. Yet it becomes easier the more confident you are of your ground. Therefore in preparing yourself for the discussion, tell yourself the following things:

1. I cannot force an admission of guilt out of my child. I can only encourage it. My object is to give him or her that opportunity.

2. The lying is my child's problem, not mine. Yet somewhere deep down he or she wants help with it.

3. I do not have to be scared of my son's or daughter's anger and bitterness. They arise from fear and guilt.

4. I can never be absolutely sure of the extent of lying or even whether there is lying at all. Therefore I must not pretend to know something I do not know or bluff my son or daughter into an admission. I am not going to play a lying game to get at the truth.

5. God knows all that happened, even though I may not. And he will never in the long run let lies go unrevealed. He cares about my child too much. It may take a lifetime, but he will be faithful.

Obviously, the older the child, the easier it will be to get across the above ideas. With a teen-ager the talk might go something like this:

"Sometimes I can tell when you're lying, Jane, and sometimes I can't. Whenever I know you're trying to fool me I'll call you on it. But if you want to deceive me, I'm not always going to be able to stop you.

"If we're to have a good relationship we've got to trust one another. Trust has to be learned. Just now I can't trust you because you've taught me not to. I want to learn to trust you again, but it'll take time. Even when you're telling me the truth I'll be thinking of all the times you've lied to me. If I act suspicious when you're telling me the truth, it's at least partly your own fault. You've fooled me so many times, Jane, that just now it's hard for me to accept all you say. I *want* to believe you, but you're going to have to teach me, and that will need time.

"I know you want to quit lying, and I know you have a problem. One thing that's bothered me is that you've only owned up when you've absolutely had to. I'll begin to know you're getting to grips with the problem when you own up to things right away, without having your arm twisted.

"There's another thing. While it's hard for you to be truthful, especially when you're scared, it's always possible to come back later and tell me you blew it, that you didn't know why you lied but that you did lie. When you do that I'll know that you are making real progress.

"I can't swear I'll never discipline you—not for lying but for whatever it is you may be lying about. This is one thing that makes it hard for you to be truthful. So when I quiz you and don't accept your word, it will be partly because I want to give you more of a chance to come clean.

"Lies separate us, Jane. They divide the family. Neither you nor I want to live in a home where neither can trust the other, yet every lie drives us further apart. But every admission of a lie does more than undo the lie. It makes me want to put my arms round you tightly because I know what a price you're paying and how much you want to put things right."

I would be giving you false hope if I told you such an interview would solve the problem. But it will be a start. What is more it can take a lot of unnecessary tension from your own life. Insofar as you let the attitude I have described represent your own heart attitude, consistently showing Jane what your attitude is, you will be opening the way for her to learn truthfulness. Jane will know where you stand—you neither condone her lying nor reject her because of it. She may also be relieved beyond measure to know you understand. It may take time. There may be many setbacks. They will be made worse by your futile attempt to force truthfulness prematurely. But if you don't, you may be surprised eventually by outbursts of truth that will make you want to cry with joy.

Out of Temptation's Way

Coping with your child's stealing, like coping with lying, must begin with yourself. I am thinking, of course, not of the occasional stealing of a younger child, but of the confirmed habit, repeated so often that it seems it will never stop. Unless you can learn peace about his or her stealing, you will be destroyed. Yet how can you?

In the next chapter I talk more of peace, but let me focus right away on acceptance. You obviously need not approve of stealing. Neither do I mean that you shrug your shoulders about it. I mean simply that you must accept the fact that Arthur has a weakness for stealing, that the weakness is Arthur's weakness, that it will not disappear by magic, but may be there for a long time yet, and that there's a limit to what

73

you can do to control it. You will help neither Arthur nor yourself by worrying yourself sick over it. Live with it.

I said there's a limit to what you can do. Nonetheless you can take some steps. If Arthur steals things at home, you can as I mentioned earlier put locks on doors, on cupboards or on drawers where valuables are kept. And you can get into the habit of keeping them locked. You must, of course, explain to Arthur and to everyone in the house why you are doing so. You don't have to call him a thief. You can recognize that his intentions may be better than his performance and tell him so. Tell him you are locking things up so that he won't be exposed to temptation. If you're a woman, never leave your purse lying around. If you're a man, watch your wallet like a hawk. Make sure you always know where your keys are, car keys included.

You say, "But I want to live in a home, not in a jail!" Possibly so. It is never pleasant to switch from a home where everyone trusts and everyone can be trusted. But a home is a place where parents must consider the moral well-being of all the members of the household. And if locks and a disciplined care of valuables are needed to shield Arthur from temptation, then you owe Arthur the extra care and protection. Locks can be a kindness when they are used for the right reasons.

A friend of mine who is a lawyer insists that locks are what create an honest society. He may be wrong, but we are fools to believe that trust produces it. Victorian homes were filled with locked doors and Victorian pockets with iron rings of skeleton keys. We look back on Victorian days as days of honesty. It is nice to reflect on idyllic states where money and property may be left lying around safely. But nostalgia will get us nowhere. Children tempted to steal need practical help and a realistic grasp of their difficulty.

You say, "But I want to be able to trust my child." Of course you do. Who can blame you? But don't let your longing cloud your judgment. Right now Arthur cannot be trusted, at least not if *being trusted* means he can withstand all degrees of temptation. Work within Arthur's limitations and don't impose conditions on him that he can't cope with merely because of your parental pride.

Trust merely confirms an already existing honesty and allows it to bloom. But the honesty has to be there to start with. Honesty is instilled by training, and even training is not always enough. Those who have temptations to steal must be protected from temptation. It is immoral to tempt weak people by exposing them to invitations they cannot resist.

Supermarkets, drugstores and department stores are calculated studies in temptation. The psychological trickery which appeals to an honest person's pocket appeals equally powerfully to a weak youngster's fingers. (It appeals to adult fingers as well, and adult shoplifters far outnumber adolescent ones!) The bright colors, the attractive display, the carefully arranged lure are all designed to undermine his resistance and overwhelm his acquisitive instincts.

I do not say that Arthur is not also to blame. I am appealing rather to your common sense and asking you to open your eyes to the fact that the dice are loaded against him—especially if his friends have learned how easy shoplifting can be and display their acquisitions to him.

Unfortunately, you can neither close down the supermarkets nor stop Arthur from visiting them. But you can keep careful watch: for extra money, for "gifts" and possessions Arthur had no realistic way of acquiring. Your heart may sink at the prospect of challenging him about them. Hassles get no easier as time goes on. But don't put them off. Ask him where he got the money or the nice gift. And let him know you are suspicious.

Once again your basic stance is: "Cool it, Arthur. No, I don't always trust you. I'll go on being suspicious until you've taught me that I can trust you. There's too much temptation around for you to find it easy to go straight, and I'm not going to assume you've got your problem licked yet."

To challenge Arthur is to help him. It is to erect fences against temptation. It tells him you're still aware. Yet if after the conversation you're not satisfied even though you've checked his statements as well as you can, don't create an impasse. You can say, "Well, you may be telling me the truth, and for both of our sakes I hope you are." Then drop the matter.

Parents tend to divide themselves into the paranoid and the naive. Assess yourself. Are you oversuspicious or are you a sucker? Whichever you are, try to assume the characteristics of the other so as to strike a balance. The hardest thing in the world, and it only comes by experience, is to know when to press an issue and when to let it ride.

Mistrust: "the seesawing between peace and no peace," as the correspondent I quoted earlier put it. I may have given you one or two practical pointers, but the quote I mention gives the real secret of inner stability for a parent grappling with anxiety over an untrustworthy child. Let me repeat it. "Then there seemed to be a real breakthrough when I was convicted that overanxiety was a sin to be repented of and that spending more time listening to the devil's 'what ifs' than to God's truths was causing the overanxiety. About that time I began studying the Psalms, unhurriedly with the Tyndale Commentary. I was startled and so very comforted by their relevance."

Notice. She was not merely glancing at Bible verses for a quick spiritual pick-me-up, but studying. Studying unhurriedly. Studying with a commentary. You don't have time? *Then make it.* If you do, you will be as startled as she was—and as deeply comforted.

5

---

*Storms
and
Peace*

Storms of unbelievable
ferocity can turn homes into disaster areas. In some households the emotional climate is rarely free from weather warnings. Instead of the gentleness and kindness that ought to
prevail, bitterness, rage, resentment and sorrow sweep
through the household. In the wake of each storm, though
calm may seem to dominate, stormy passions continue to rage
inside the hearts of individual family members.

Anger is inevitable at times, and freedom to express angry
feelings is both healthy and desirable. But the storms I speak
of are unhealthy and destructive. Where do they come from
and how can they be avoided? Is it possible to avoid them? Or
are they inevitable, given the mix of incompatible personalities in some families? Let us begin by observing the storms.

Tornadoes of Violence

We read of a child battering. We are sickened. So shocking a
rage not only dismays us, it leaves us uncomprehending.
Some of us are bewildered by *any* anger directed at children,
feeling it is as unnecessary as it is cruel. Yet some parents who

give way to anger are bewildered themselves. Their rage often takes them by surprise and humiliates them, bursting like an angry sea over breakwaters they have built to contain it. They grow to be as afraid of their anger as their children are—and deeply ashamed. Some nights they are drawn into their children's bedrooms to stare with inarticulate tenderness at little round faces whose air of innocence silently reproaches them. They may shake their heads and sigh, mutter pointless regrets or stoop to plant a futile kiss on a soft, sleeping cheek.

The bewilderment of such parents is greater than that of their critics. They alone know the frustration of playing host to such incongruous feelings as tenderness and rage. "How can it be," they ask themselves as they stand at the foot of the child's bed, "that I felt and acted as I did?" So to rage and tenderness are added guilt, shame and perhaps self-pity. Their shoulders sag and their faces stare down at the floor.

It does not surprise ethologists that parents may experience both rage and tenderness toward the same child. Konrad Lorenz in his book *On Aggression* describes the behavior of gray lag geese toward their young.[1] Evidently the birds do not experience vision in precisely the way we do. Instead of perceiving the form of an object, they see a combination of form and movement. Small moving creatures (mice, rats, snakes) are attacked with murderous rage. The rage has a purpose. It keeps the young safe.

Only the incessant cheeping of the young birds assures their own safety. The cheeping is a cue, switching off the mother's rage. Just as the sight of a sleeping child may waken protective feelings in parents, so the sound of the cheeping inhibits rage in parent birds. If you bind the chicks' beaks so they cannot cheep or take away the mother bird's hearing (this has actually been done), she will no longer distinguish between her young and other small moving creatures but will attack and kill indiscriminately. The cue has been destroyed.

The rage cannot be controlled. If you give her mechanical young with a tape-recorded "cheep" inside them, she will respond as a parent should. Turn off the tape recorder, and she will rush at the toys in a fury.

Ethologists would explain human parental rage in the same way as the rage of a gray lag goose. It has (or perhaps once had) a protective function and is inhibited by certain characteristics in young children—the roundness of their heads, the clumsiness and uncoordination of their movements. A one-year-old has only to toddle rockily toward you, stagger, sit down with a bump and smile, and your aggression dies inside you just as the parent bird's aggression dies at the sound of a cheep. What ethologists are less able to tell us is why the human mechanism goes wrong and how explosive anger can be controlled.

Annette was a black-haired, slender beauty of thirty who came to see me because of her anger with Karen, her second child, a daughter of six months. She twisted a handkerchief between her fingers throughout the interview and her eyes looked haunted. A Christian? Yes, she was a Christian. She believed that Christ was God and that he had died to forgive her sins. She had been baptized in the Spirit and spoke in tongues. She knew God forgave her for Christ's sake, yet how could he forgive her cruelty to Karen?

I asked how cruel she had been. She bit her lip and stared at me. "Her little butt's all bruised," she said. "She's always been a colicky baby, and we've lost a lot of sleep because of her. I . . . I just can't stand her crying. She's O.K. if I pick her up, but as soon as I put her down she starts in again. And Bill never helps. He just sits around doing nothing when he's at home. I'll be doing the dishes and Benny, he's two, will be into everything while Karen lies there and screams. Bill just won't discipline Benny and he leaves Karen to cry. I can stand it only so long."

"Is that when you spank Karen?"

"No. It's when I'm alone that I spank her. She never seems to stop crying."

"How hard do you spank?"

There was a long pause.

"Sometimes I shake her—hard. I'm so ashamed."

She was looking down now at the twisted handkerchief. "It scares her. She sobs. Once or twice I've actually thrown her—just into the crib—not on the floor or anything. I feel awful. She's so tiny and helpless. I pray for forgiveness but I feel God can't possibly forgive me. I don't feel like he even hears me."

I suggested that Annette take Karen to the emergency room to be checked. X rays showed several fractures including a fractured skull, fractured ribs and a fractured right arm. With Annette's and Bill's consent I arranged for temporary custody of Karen until Annette's outbursts could be helped.

I don't think I have ever seen shame such as Annette displayed when she told me about the x rays. The knowledge that she was a Christian greatly magnified it. She had previously known a tendency to beat her first child and had resorted to fasting and prayer, to public confession of her sin in church and earnest attempts to yield herself constantly to the Holy Spirit. She had attended several conventions with her husband and had consulted several preachers, some of whom claimed to have cast demons out of her. A psychiatrist had given her tranquilizing medication though she did not appear to suffer from any clearly defined emotional illness. Slowly she got over the problem until Karen arrived, and then again, during the first six months of Karen's life, she had made serious attempts to get help, mainly from pastors and preachers.

If you have a problem like Annette's and especially if it concerns a small child, get help. Don't wait around hoping things will improve. You and your child are in danger. Go to a physician or a counselor you can trust and say, "I can't control my urge to beat Jimmy, and I'm afraid I might do him serious harm. I need help." Don't rest until you get help, help *from people with experience with this specific problem.* Most children's hospitals have clinics for parents who lose control during discipline.

Annette (along with Bill) got the help she needed from therapy for couples and from a godly pastor. Karen was boarded temporarily in a foster home where Annette could visit and feed her almost daily. After a few months when it seemed that Annette's problem was overcome, Karen returned home. Several years have passed and Annette has had no relapses. The family is happy and Karen is doing well in school.

Hurricanes of Words
Parents express their anger in many ways besides physical violence. Raised voices are more common than raised fists. Insults, criticisms, slammed doors and flying dishes may all attest to parental anger. It is easy to condemn wrathful parents but not so easy to help them forsake wrath. The more they strive to control their outbursts, the fiercer the outbursts may become; the greater the parental remorse, the worse the subsequent behavior; the higher and nobler the parents' ideals, the more humiliating are their defeats. Overeating, sexual indiscretions, drunkenness all have their peculiar pains. But a burst of rage that wounds someone I love or that destroys an object I cherish is unequaled in its power to torture.

"I begin some days," one parent told me, "with an absolute determination not to let an angry word cross my lips. I tell myself there's no reason to say the things I do and that I don't have to say one word I don't want to. Yet halfway through the morning I find myself listening to an unbelievable stream of abuse pouring from my own lips. It happens constantly."

Not all parents care. Some destroy their children with

cutting words or blows and experience no remorse. Yet others are acutely sensitive to the pain they inflict. They would much sooner hurt themselves than harm their children.

"I can't bear the way she looks at me—hurt and scared. And I know I've done it again. I've destroyed a bit more of her," a mother wrote me. "That look is worse than a beating from my husband. I love Jean and I really want her to grow up feeling loved and safe, yet here I am scaring the hell out of her."

A father wrote, "I want Ken to love me. I need his love more than ever since [my wife] Mary left, yet I'm the one who's destroying it by the way I treat him. I get pretty desperate at times."

Many Sunday-school teachers and pastors drive to church on Sunday morning already defeated by memories of the vicious words they spat at another family member at the breakfast table. Once spoken the words cannot be erased. Anger subsides; shame, guilt, depression and a sense of hopelessness replace it.

"I was mad at my wife not at my oldest daughter Marie," a pastor told me a few weeks ago. "Sunday morning's always a hassle and Emily never stops nagging the kids. I was trying to concentrate on a last bit of sermon preparation when Marie talked back to her. I tore out of the study and said things to my daughter that I'll never forget. How can I preach self-control to others when I do things like that? Ought I to quit the ministry?"

A psychologist I know told me of her own maternal behavior. "As an infant Daryl was colicky and had no delay tolerance with regard to feeding. His incessant screaming led to my husband and I accusing each other of not knowing how to handle the child. This led to shouting matches between us. Even today, whenever Daryl begins to act up we often respond by accusing each other of doing something to make him act this way. In general we can be on good terms yet in a matter of moments following an outburst by Daryl we find ourselves shouting at each other."

Worst of all is what I mentioned earlier, the pain of witnessing the hurt of someone my anger has needlessly wounded and of knowing I am destroying a relationship that is precious to me. A social worker employed by a children's aid society wrote me that he shouted at his own son when he was still quite young even though he was aware that the boy was terrified by it.

Parents must of course be willing to be misunderstood by children. Discipline demands that parents not be controlled by their children's tears. Clear consciences and the knowledge that they are acting in the child's best interests can sustain parents. Properly executed, discipline normally cements a relationship. But vicious, hurtful words can destroy it, and it is hard at times to know who suffers more, parent or child, because of them.

Wrong anger is a weed which once sown in the family soil springs up in unexpected places. It is a troublesome weed to control, spreading to every family member since angry habits are learned by example. And if there is one thing that angers parents, it is displays of anger in their children, a fact which produces situations which would be amusing if they were not tragic.

Tony, who has learned angry outbursts from his siblings and parents, tears his workbook up in a fit of temper over a "stupid" assignment. His action angers his brother who berates him loudly until the two are almost ready for a fistfight. Barbara, their older sister, moves with hostile efficiency to settle the dispute and to tell them both "to shut their big mouths." But Barbara discovers she has only added fuel to the fire whose flames roar all the louder. Mother is horrified. She has told Barbara repeatedly not to interfere with the boys' quarrels because *that* only makes matters worse. So she runs downstairs to give her daughter a piece of her mind. But scarcely has she begun when her husband, convinced that his wife is too critical of her daughter, adds his voice to the hubbub.

In the heat of the moment words are spoken which are regretted when it is too late. The verbal conflagration is out of hand. One boy runs in terror from the house, another stares wide eyed at his angry, shouting parents while the daughter slams a door to listen to the fracas from her bedroom.

It is their third row in as many days. The family seems to be perpetually at flash point. A spark of anger over a minor incident catches the whole family in a spreading explosion that threatens to blow them apart. As one teen-ager said to me, half joking, half in bitterness, "It only takes my kid brother to kick the dog and in two minutes the whole family is at one another's throats." Surprisingly, fighting family members usually live in terror of losing one another's support. They know they need one another. Much of the fighting seems to arise from this very fear so that angry flames erupt continually among them.

It seems to make little difference how "spiritual" or how idealistic a family is. The desire to display love and courtesy is not enough. It almost seems that the more an insecure family yearns for closeness, the more explosive it becomes. The parents are the key to the situation and almost always they know it. But knowing, far from helping, only discourages them because of years of defeat.

Not all parental anger is on the surface. Some of it festers behind a haggard face, keeping a man or woman staring at the ceiling of a darkened bedroom or turning restlessly in search of peace.

From the diary of a writer who was disturbed over her adolescent son's stealing, I was allowed to read the following:

1 A.M.

My purse. I could have sworn I'd taken the money out of it and locked it in the drawer. But did I? Perhaps I put it in

my coat pocket, because I was. . . . No, it's not there. Where
could it be? It's not the forty dollars I care about.

Why do we have to go through this all the time?

I must have left it in my purse. But, no, I've looked there
twice. My own fault. I should have been more careful. But
why do I have to watch my every move? Why must I never
forget where I put things down? Why do I have to keep an
endless check on my keys? Sooner or later I make a mistake
—and sure enough he spots it and the money disappears.

But maybe I'm jumping to conclusions. Surely I *must*
have locked the cash away. Perhaps I left it in the family
room, I remember stopping there. . . .

Guess I'm fooling myself. I know what's happened. I'm
not letting myself think it yet, but I know. Why am I trembling? Why do I always get this sick shaking inside my
tummy and want to sit down?

It feels like rage. My hands are shaking. I thought he was
over it. Oh, God, when will it end? Must this go on forever?
I'm angry and confused. I wish I didn't have to go on living
like this. Does it have to be? Does home have to be a security
lockup with us always having to watch his every move?

I feel mad at God. Why does he not stop this tension?
Why does it continue endlessly? I know he cares for my boy.
I know I should thank him for his faithfulness to me. It's
not all meaningless.

My hands have stopped shaking. I feel depressed—but I
have more peace now. The basic rules haven't changed.
God is still there. I'll go on. Meanwhile there's the show-
down to face—and perhaps the spiritual help to give my
boy.

1 P.M. [the following day]

I found the money. He hadn't taken it.

I asked him, of course, and there was something unde-
finable—friendly—something about his denial which itself
was convincing. So my turmoil was all over nothing. I

guess this is all part of learning about God's peace.

Perhaps it is better that a person's anger hurt no one but him or herself, but it would be better still if the anger could be defused. Inner anger can cause physical harm. Repressed anger may cause you to break out in eczema. Some forms of arthritis and a number of other ills may be traced to it. Curiously, those parents who are the least conscious of anger are the ones in whom it does the most physical damage.

Some angry parents smile perpetually. They may even be vivacious, cheerful, lacing their conversations with frequent ejaculations of praise to God. I am moved by their brave efforts to keep their grief and their anger at bay, but I notice that in some the cheerfulness seems brittle, the smiles too set and the expletives of joy mechanical. Such people deny that they are angry. Yet they complain that when things began to go wrong at home that their ulcers, their headaches, their eczema or whatever began to act up.

An army major discovered his nineteen-year-old son was a practicing homosexual. Within three weeks he broke out in an inflamed, itching rash which continued to afflict him for months. His wife complained of frequent abdominal pain. Six months after the discovery she was hospitalized when she hemorrhaged from a gastric ulcer. The major and his wife were both quiet people who expressed little feeling and who exercised self-control. Neither admitted to feelings of anger.

"It was a terrible shock," the major stated. "What made it worse was that we couldn't talk to him. He walked out of the house a couple of weeks after we found out. But we just committed the whole thing to the Lord. Anger? No, I can't say I felt any anger. I was *hurt,* but I wasn't angry."

His wife's story was similar. "Yes, it was a shock. I'd always been so close to Ron and suddenly there was this wall there and anything I said seemed to upset him. The worst part is not knowing where he is. But even about that I've learned to praise and thank the Lord."

At the advice of the major's physician both went for counseling to a skilled psychologist. At first they resisted the idea that anger was a problem. They had not been conscious of anger and had therefore assumed that no anger was present. Little by little the psychologist put them in touch with some of their feelings, feelings they had never before allowed themselves to experience. Only then did the major's eczema, which had previously resisted all his physician's attempts at healing, finally disappear.

Springs of Anger
Anger has too many causes to be dealt with in a single chapter. The examples I shall give are only a selection from a longer list.

Displaced anger is directed toward one person or situation though it was caused by another. A woman angry with her boss may say nothing while in the office but will express her anger toward her husband or children later on. A man who is angry with his mother-in-law may kick the door or the dog. In any organization the person who is lowest on the totem pole absorbs the greatest amount of punishment simply because displaced anger is normally expressed downward. Anger directed toward children, then, may sometimes have nothing to do with the children themselves.

Pressure-cooker anger sometimes builds up in people who are not assertive (not able to express their wishes and feelings clearly and appropriately). They may get into the habit of letting frustration build to a point where they can no longer control it. At that point a trivial incident will produce an explosion. In the same way parents who are afraid to be firm with their children, even though they dislike the way the children behave, may be alternately easygoing and explosive.

Anger which can result from mental illness is characterized by outbursts of rage. Even simple anxiety makes some people explosive. Worries about finances, about employment, about illness, in-law conflicts and about any number of minor difficulties may all contribute to an increase in angry outbursts. Loss of sleep may be a factor, as may specific fears or a sense of insecurity.

Though I cannot deal thoroughly with all forms of explosive anger, perhaps I can limit myself to some forms which offer more hope of benefiting from an understanding of spiritual principles. It may be that you are overwhelmed by anger of a kind not easily dealt with by a change of pace or a break. You may have no understanding of the cause of your anger, or you may know the cause but be powerless to deal with it or to find a solution in what I have to say in the rest of this chapter. In that case it would be wise to look for help from a trained counselor, psychologist or other professional. Anger is a fire in your bosom which does not only damage others but damages and hurts you, the angry person. Try to overcome your embarrassment and seek for help, for your own sake as well as for your family's.

Disappointed Expectations
Among the many causes of parental explosions are two common and closely related attitudes. Both have to do with unrealistic expectations, first of your children and second of your ability to control your children's behavior.

Disappointed expectations make us all angry. If I expect traffic to move briskly on the way to the airport and it doesn't, I get upset. If in spite of traffic difficulties I get to the airport in time only to find my plane has left, I am angry. In the same way, if I expect my children to behave in certain ways and they don't, then again I am inclined to become inflamed.

Tragically, many parents have unrealistic hopes and expectations of their children, about their careers as well as about everyday things. If you expect Veronica to stop picking her nose the first time you ask, and if Veronica goes on picking her nose, the stage is set for an explosion. Under such circumstances a tense parent faces two possible solutions: (1) to control his or her temper every time Veronica picks her nose; (2) not to expect Veronica to get over her habit right away. Solution number two is the better one. If you don't have to cope with unrealistic expectations, you have less anger to control. If you can accept the fact that unpleasant as the habit is it will probably take Veronica a little while to get it out of her system and that she may well display her nose picking when you entertain guests, you will not be so tense.

Accepting such a solution may not be easy. It will involve visualizing all the unpleasant situations in which Veronica displays her digital expertise, realizing that the earth will not come to an end whatever lapses she may have. Once you can accept this you will begin to make progress. But it will take practice, practice picturing Veronica picking her nose in front of guests, practice reminding yourself that Veronica is more important to you than they are and that she sometimes forgets. This kind of practice constitutes an exercise in putting yourself in Veronica's shoes. Habits are habits. You may have one or two yourself that you have difficulty controlling—like getting mad.

Please understand that I am not recommending that you ignore Veronica's problem. We are talking now not about how to stop her picking her nose but how not to get mad when she does.

Disappointed expectations, then, may surprise us into explosions. But expectations sit so quietly on our shoulders, so lightly around our belts and seclude themselves so unobtrusively in our pockets that we are unaware of their presence. Unless, check list in hand, we inspect ourselves to bring hidden expectations to light, they will victimize us mercilessly. Let us look at a few of the commoner ones.

Have I been expecting that home will always be a haven of refuge and peace? Many of us do. The expectation is understandable but hardly realistic. In any case it is the parents' responsibility

to make the home a haven of peace not for their own benefit but for their family's. It is the parent birds who line the nest
with down.

But all question of rights aside, home will not always be a
quiet haven. And if fathers and mothers, weary from struggles
of the day, expect to have peace at home, they are in for dis-
appointments from time to time.

*Have I been expecting more than my child is capable of, accomplish-
ments beyond his or her stage of development?* Children mature at
different rates. Bowel and bladder control, motor skills, a
sense of responsibility and even puberty cannot be predicted
with precision. Not all small children walk at twelve months or
talk at twenty-four months. Flowers do not open simultaneously in spring. What am I expecting of my child? Is it
realistic? If it is not, my child and I may both suffer needless
distress because of my anger at not encountering what I
thought I had a right to expect.

*Am I expecting behavior radically different from that of other
children of the same age?* Different table manners? A different
degree of room tidiness? A different attitude to haircuts and
bathing frequency? A different degree of forgetfulness? Or
of truthfulness? A lower frequency of sibling hassles and
rivalries? A greater immunity to temptation?

We use the word *expect* in different senses of course. When
we tell a child, "I expect you to sit up straight at the table!" we
are really saying that we want the child to do so and that we
don't intend to let him or her get away with anything less. But
that is not the kind of expecting we're talking about. We are
dealing with unconscious or half-conscious assumptions, with
what we thought or imagined should and would happen.

Naturally we want to see certain standards observed by our
children. Quite rightly we aim at such standards which may
indeed be higher than those we observe in our children's con-
temporaries (for once again we are not dealing with the question of whether we ought to let standards slide but with how to

cope with our feelings when they do). It is a mistake to under-estimate an enemy, and if the enemy is contemporary cul-ture, then we are doubly foolish to do so. Our expectations will be dashed and we will be angered because we have been living in a dream world.

Think of it from the child's point of view. He may know what you want. He may even, at times, want it too. But know-ing and doing are not the same. Our children are powerfully influenced by culture, are gripped by habits and, like us, have to grapple with fierce temptation. Not all bad behaviors rep-resent deliberate disobedience, rebellion or stubborness. And even those that do may be the end result of an intense inner struggle. If we are not going to be thrown by their undesirable behavior, we must take hard and frequent looks at them, must try to understand what they are coping with so that we know what to expect.

Some of our expectations may arise from our selfishness. Although we assure ourselves that we want only our children's good, our expectations may in reality have a lot to do with our personal pride and comfort. If this is the case then our anger will be adulterated with bitterness and resentment. It is well to look not only at what we expect of our children but also why we have such expectations.

Dictators and Diplomats
Closely related to the matter of our expectations is that of control. In theory parents steadily relax control as their chil-dren grow older. In practice we may have difficulty relin-quishing control because of personal fears and hang-ups. In chapter nine I speak at length about relinquishment, but for the moment let me draw attention to the relation between control and angry outbursts.

It doesn't bother me so much now, but when I was younger I had a problem during my daily devotions. Whenever I opened my eyes I would notice something in the room that needed to be changed: a picture on the wall was lopsided; a piece of paper was lying on the floor; the bedcover was not straight. Whatever the problem was I could not resist a compulsion to rectify matters. Indeed I could not go on praying or studying until I had done so. Efforts to remedy my compulsiveness were unavailing. I had to have everything in apple-pie order before I could proceed. I could not relax until I had controlled my environment and was comfortable with it.

Now consider environment not only in terms of tilted pictures, paper-littered floors and untidy bedspreads but in terms of too much noise or too much movement. Many of us feel a compulsion to create a certain emotional environment. But whereas pictures and bedspreads can be straightened and paper picked up, children, not being inanimate objects, are less easy to tidy away.

We are back, of course, to the problem of irritating habits, like Veronica and her nose and Tony with his elbows on the table. Because our desire to stop Veronica picking her nose or to make Tony keep his elbows off the table sometimes arises from our neurotic need to keep the place tidy, it produces in us an unrealistic attempt at control. We expect Veronica and Tony to respond as easily and accommodatingly as the inanimate articles in my bedroom. We may not even be thinking of the children themselves but only of the offending behavior they give rise to. I am sure that if the picture on my wall had persisted in jogging itself crooked the moment I knelt down again, eventually I might well have exploded with rage. And that is just what we do with Veronica and Tony.

Our need to control children is not always a neurotic compulsion, however. Sometimes it arises from a mindset, an inner attitude determining our reactions. One consists in the belief that it is a parent's job *to create desirable character and habits in a child and that any failure to do so represents parental mismanagement.* Such a mindset produces tension. Every time a child does something he or she shouldn't, something deep inside the parent says, "I'm losing control! I've blown it again!"

The parent may only be conscious of an uprush of fear and rage or of a physical or verbal outburst, followed after a while by depression. If the mindset was different, the sequence would not take place. But mindsets are not easily changed. This particular mindset represents the false and unrealistic belief that the molding of a child's character must be the work of the parents. It fails, as I mentioned in chapter three, to sufficiently account for the freedom of the child or to allow for the fallibility of the parent.

Usually this is a mindset produced by the parents' own up-bringing and experiences. It has grown slowly to dominate their thinking and their wills. It includes a feeling of omnipotence, "I can and I must control the child!" But it also includes fears. "If I fail there will be tragedy. At all costs I *must* maintain control."

Parents never hear the words, but they do experience the emotions that go along with them. Guilt and remorse add to the problem. In her determination a mother may screw up her will to such a pitch of intensity that her reflexes are hair-trigger sensitive.

The mindset that leads to this could be summarized as follows: God gave me children who now belong to me. I love them and am going to pray and work to bring them up well. I shall try to train them to be a credit both to God and to our family, as well as to be happy themselves. If, trusting in God, I "do my stuff" as a parent, all will be well. I shall only have myself to blame if I fail.

The above mindset is, I believe, mistaken. A second is better: My children are a temporary trust from God. They are "mine" only in the sense that God counts on me to love them, discipline them, train them. They were not given me so that I could boast of their good points any more than I should be ashamed of their failures. I am temporarily watching over the development of other human beings who rightly belong to

God, whose destiny will ultimately be decided between each child and God alone.

A parent with the first mindset takes on a greater degree of responsibility than a parent with the second. Some of the responsibility is needless and tension producing. Our objective must not be to control but to offer our parental help. It is true that we must teach obedience, but we cannot control the rate at which children learn obedience. We may only provide the best conditions we can for them to learn. The rest is up to them under the hand of God. We must chastise. We must even punish. But our aim will not be to control everything that happens. It will be to provide guidelines. When a child strays beyond the guidelines, we must seek to bring the child back.

The more energy you use exerting control, whether that control is over your children or over yourself and your impatience, the less energy you will have for living and coping. If you were full of peace, there would be no anger to control and therefore more energy for living. Putting the lid on a fight may be good but it is not enough. It is a Band-Aid approach to family conflict. It may result in less noise, greater order and less danger of bruises, but if resentment and bitterness still seethe below the surface, the gain is limited. Control has been established because explosive pressure has been bottled up both in you and in your children, making the control costly and unstable. If control depends on your skills as a diplomat or your authority as a dictator, you will have to be constantly on the alert to maintain control. You will have to watch for every spurt of flame that heralds a forest fire and stamp it out (if you are a dictator) or rush in with water (if you are a diplomat).

Oil on Troubled Waters
We speak of "pouring oil on troubled waters." The metaphor springs from the curious way oil makes tumultuous waves subside by changing the surface tension of water and reduc-

ing the effects of wind. Rescue operations from wrecked ships have occasionally been made easier and safer by pouring oil on the sea surrounding them.

To become a source of peace is to become oil on troubled waters. Becoming oil is not a technique by which you psych your family into tranquility. To do so is to play the diplomat, the very thing I am suggesting we supersede. To be oil demands more than saying helpful things or adopting helpful stances. It means to enjoy peace yourself, a peace which must spring from your own experience.

You may have come across people who spread a sense of relaxation round them. Tension melts when they enter a room. Matters which had us trembling or biting our fingernails suddenly seem trifles. The sun comes out when such people start to speak.

The question we must ask is not, "How do they do it?" It is not what they do that matters but what they *are*. They are themselves at peace. And because they are at peace they become sources of peace to others. We sense their inner rest and are both grateful for it and reassured by it. To be a source of peace then means to be so at peace within yourself that you are not ruffled by storms. Instead a sense of peace communicates itself to troubled people around you.

If you were to take a mild tranquilizer half an hour before a family explosion, you might exude peace yourself. Your anxieties would lessen, leaving you serene and gentle. Inner worries would seem trivial. Conflict in the family would frighten you less, and you could approach problems calmly as long as the pill lasted. Sensing this, and provided you hadn't taken too much, tension would begin to subside in the rest of the family, but at the cost of exposing you to a bad and dangerous habit.

I do not recommend tranquilizers for family conflicts. You need a genuine peace, the kind that makes dogs wag their tails and babies hold out their arms to you. Nor is the peace I recommend an "oh-it-doesn't-matter" peace, a peace that lets vital matters slide or that fails to come to grips with family problems. It must condone neither irresponsibility nor escapism but must be a peace arising from an inner assurance that all is well—the clear-eyed peace of a person who is in touch with God.

When you are upset, irritated, angry, you cannot contribute to peace in others. But when your spirit is quiet and at rest, then when you intervene in a hassle your peace will reassure others, diminishing their resentment. Move in with a belligerent attitude and you may succeed in controlling expressions of hostility in your family, but you will never solve the resentments and bitterness that gave rise to the storm in the first place. A meek and a quiet spirit is of great price in God's sight and an equally priceless resource in family life.

To become a center of peace in your family is *to accept the fact that trouble is bound to come* but that the trouble does not necessarily mean you have failed as a parent. There will be sibling rivalries. Conflicts will arise as children learn to respect one another's property or as they struggle to cope with their understandable jealousies of older, more gifted or more fortunate brothers and sisters. The jealousies and resentments may not be good. But they will occur. You must accept that. They are part of a process by which children come to terms with the real world inside their own families. To accept the fact that these things will occur does not mean to approve them. It means not being thrown into a tizzy by them, recognizing that it would be very surprising if they did not occur.

To be a center of peace means *to have the capacity to take disturbing traits and behavior* in other family members without being inwardly upset. It means having realistic expectations of children at different stages in their development. If you expect two-year-old Susie to sit through a church service on a hard pew like a wax dummy, you will never be at peace for Susie is not made of wax. Experts differ over what children can be trained to do at different ages, but to expect more than they are capable of, or to expect them to carry out tasks they have never been trained to carry out is to create inner turmoil for yourself. Live in a real world if you would have inner peace.

To be a center of peace in the family means *to be free from fear about the family.* Peace and fear cannot coexist. I sat in a family conference a little while ago at which family members tried to get to the root of their problem. It was a large, three-generation family whose members longed for closeness. Several of the members, men and women, wept at the conference deploring the quarrels that had driven them apart. Slowly it became evident that one of the biggest factors in their explosions was fear—paradoxically a fear that the family would be torn apart. They were all striving so hard to keep the family together that their very fear of failure made them doubly tense. All of them were conscious that they needed the family, that they needed one another. Yet all of them were terrified that their relationship was too fragile to last and that at any moment an explosion would destroy the family. Their fear put them under such tension that it was virtually impossible for them to avoid explosions. The discovery of their fears began to pave the way for a less troubled relationship.

To have peace yourself will mean *to stop demanding that other family members be centers of peace.* It means, most especially, that you must not count on your spouse for your own peace. Many spouses are centers of peace. It will be delightful if yours is too. But if you expect and demand that someone else supply the family's peace, you will lose your peace the moment that person becomes agitated. Other people's anger must be powerless to shake you. You must be prepared to be the center of family peace.

To be a center of peace means *to recognize that you cannot eradicate the sins and weaknesses of other family members.* You may, if it is appropriate to do so, counsel or discipline them, but the recurrence or nonrecurrence of their sins and failures lies beyond your power. Your family will continue to display weakness and sin. This may grieve you, but it should not surprise and need not dismay you.

A Lighthouse of Peace

So far, we have discussed both interpersonal peace (peace among different family members) and intrapersonal (inner) peace. We all know that when peace exists among members of our families everyone feels more inner peace. My thesis has been that the influence is two way. I have been encouraging you to find intrapersonal peace. I have suggested some attitudes which are inconsistent with inner peace. But crucial to this is the fundamental source of peace and how to discover it.

Whereas I have discussed two kinds of peace, the Bible discusses three types, all of which are related. In addition to inner peace and peace between one person and another it speaks of the source of both: peace between God and us. No one can know the depths of peace who does not have peace with God. No one can be a center, a source, or better, a channel of peace who does not fully enjoy peace with God.

You may have felt dissatisfied as you read over some of the attitudes to family matters that are inconsistent with inner peace, sensing that such a peace might be elusive or even unattainable for you. If you are a Christian, you are probably familiar with biblical descriptions of inner peace but may have slowly come to regard it as a scarcely attainable state that only athletic souls experience. If you do not presently enjoy the peace of God, never mind. Let us windowshop and view the peace that is on display, considering to whom it was offered. If we find such peace was only for psychologically stable and sophisticated people or for people who were shielded from conflict, then it will be little use to us.

"Peace I leave with you; my peace I give to you; not as the world gives do I give to you. Let not your hearts be troubled, neither let them be afraid," Jesus told the apostles as they were about to face a tumultuous reception in a hostile world (Jn. 14:27). The peace Christ gave them did not shelter them *from* the tumults, accusations or persecution, but it sustained them *in* them. The Jesus who spoke peace to them was the same Jesus who from a wildly rocking fishing boat had shouted into the teeth of a gale, "Peace! Be still!" bringing its furies to an astonished halt and causing the impassioned waters to lap meekly around the sides of the boat. His word to their hearts was no less effective than his word in the storm. He gave them peace, *his* peace, with which they subsequently strode through demonic storms of raging hatreds.

Being the Prince of Peace he could say to them, "I have said this to you, that in me you may have peace. In the world you have tribulation; but be of good cheer, I have overcome the world" (Jn. 16:33). In Christ, peace. In the world, tribulation. But Christ has overcome the world. The peace he spoke of was not a sort of spiritual tranquilizer, sedating the nervous systems of jumpy disciples. It was the peace of a strong man in control. The peace the disciples were to experience *arose from their relationship with him and from his relationship with the world.*

Picture yourself in a well-built lighthouse founded on solid rock. Huge waves might crash and mighty gales might scream around it, yet inside the lighthouse is peace. Out in the storm you would be buffeted, bruised and soaked to the skin. But the lighthouse is overcoming the storm in the same way that Jesus overcomes the world. The rain may dash itself against the walls and the windows but from inside you need have no concern.

Such is the peace Jesus offers that Paul speaks of it as, "The peace of God, which passes all understanding" (Phil. 4:7). "Great peace" is the psalmist's description (Ps. 119:165).

The quality of the inner peace you need then is great peace, peace that goes beyond human comprehension, the peace by which Jesus could reduce a storm to gentleness or send

unsophisticated disciples carefree into a world of hatred. Such
a peace is meant to possess the heart of Christians, surrounding them with the kind of wall against which disturbing ideas
and circumstances dash themselves impotently. Why do so
few of us possess it? How can our frightened and wrathful
spirits be subdued by it?

Peace with God

To experience the peace *of* God you must know peace *with*
God. And peace with God implies that a state of hostility between God and you is at an end.

Many Christians are deeply confused about their relationship with God. Their theology is divorced from their experience. Their heads can assert truths that their hearts do
not appreciate. They know that Jesus, by his sacrificial death,
has paid for their peace with God and that their own faith in
Christ secures that peace for them. Yet their consciences
haunt them. Specters of sins past and present rise to drive
them from the throne of grace so that they stand ashamed
and at a distance from God wondering how they may get right
with him again. They know, in theory at least, that all their
sins are paid for, that God is well pleased with the sacrifice of
his Beloved One, satisfied that all accounts have been settled.
Yet they feel something is wrong.

How could Annette know peace with God when she was
told what the x rays on Karen showed? How can parents who
beat their children brutally or who scream destructive rage at
them know peace with God? Is God not concerned about such
sins?

God is indeed concerned about them. He abhors them. If
brutality against the helpless seems appalling to us, it appalls
God far more. His own unceasing, immutable hostility is directed against it. He accepts no excuse for it. If you are an
angry parent who has brutalized your children by your lack
of control, then be assured that God is extremely concerned.

What you have done is evil. God is concerned for your children and more horrified than you are at the way you cause them suffering. He deplores what you have done. Yet he loved you so deeply that he sought a way to come to terms with your dilemma.

So his anger is no longer directed at you. He who saw from the beginning what your undisciplined temper would do, directed his righteous rage against his Son. What Jesus suffered we shall probably never know, but his suffering included God's retribution for the cruelty you have been exhibiting against your children.

There is no way you can atone for your brutality. To try to atone is to belittle what Christ willingly suffered on your behalf. With the Father's anger against you appeased, he bids you come to him and know that he understands your distress and failure but that he has put your sin behind his back.

Most parents try to atone for wrongs they do to their children by making up to them or by showing extra kindness and warmth. To make amends in this way is both bad for the children and bad for the parents. It is bad for the children in that they are subjected to seesaw swings in their parents' moods. It is bad for the parents in that it represents an inadequate sop to conscience. To atone for my misdeeds is to get even with my conscience by performing what the writer to the Hebrews calls "dead works" (Heb. 9:14). It is to offer to God my own performance alongside the sacrifice of his Son. It is to declare Christ's sacrifice inadequate.

I do not say that parents should ignore their misdeeds to their children. An honest apology, a forthright admission of wrong courteously and clearly explained to the child (but not a covert please-go-on-loving-me plea) can only do good. But the acknowledgment of wrong is not atonement. It does not lessen the crime I have committed, the stain of which can only be cleansed by blood. The sin must be called to mind in the presence of God.

There is a right and a wrong remembering of sin just as there is a right and wrong way to meditate on it. You can wallow in self-loathing, heaping abuse on yourself and forcing yourself to squirm before the ugliness of your character and your sins. This is the wrong way to meditate on sin. It will only lead you to despair or to renewed efforts at improvement, efforts which are doomed to failure unless the root cause is dealt with.

Or you can view your foulness dispassionately, inquiring, "Why am I like this? If I can find what makes me so, perhaps I can correct it." At first this would seem a more wholesome meditating upon sin, offering some hope of cure. Yet in practice it seldom does. There are exceptions to be sure. Self-understanding is not to be despised. Yet even when it is achieved it is often unhelpful.

Let us suppose you discover that you are angry with your children because your father was angry with you when you were a child. How much will your discovery help? In practice usually very little. The knowledge may comfort you. But it is unlikely to have much impact on your behavior. Or let us suppose you find you are angry because you lack the love and patience to pay attention to your children, that you are yourself love-starved. It is good to know you are starved of love. But from where will you get the love you need? How will your own need to be loved be satisfied? Self-understanding is at best a partial help. I do not recommend meditating on your sins for such a reason.

Meditation is right when it causes you to worship. If when you contemplate your sin you are able to perceive the wonder of God's kindness in forgiving it and to marvel at the wisdom of a God who forgives it justly, if his divine plan, his incredible longsuffering and patience or the depths of his mercy awaken awe and thanksgiving in you, then you do well to meditate on your sin. Look at it in all its horror and know that the Savior knew of it before he embraced his crucifixion. Contemplate the number of times you have fallen into the same sin and marvel at (but do not presume on) his patience and grace.

The peace *of* God is (among other things) a subjective experience. Peace *with* God is an objective reality providing the basis for the subjective experience. To grasp the nature of your peace with God it is necessary to go back to Scripture and allow the Holy Spirit to flood your mind with an understanding of what Christ has done to establish that peace for you.

Peace means that God and you, you who behave so shabbily to your children, are reconciled (Rom. 5:10). It means that for Christ's sake God accepts you just as you are. It means that he is well pleased with you, indeed that he takes delight in you now that Christ has purchased your redemption. It means that you need have no shame before him but may approach him boldly (Heb. 10:21-22). It means that he has, because of the blood of Christ, freely forgiven any of your parental failures, rages and cruelties that you are willing to acknowledge (Eph. 4:32; 1 Jn. 2:12).

To know such peace is to know that you are loved and accepted. And to know oneself loved and accepted is to experience a melting away of inner frustrations and angers. I have never known a greater freedom from anger than immediately following my awareness of how greatly I am loved and how freely forgiven.

There is no firmer or broader base for inner peace than to be assured of peace with God. Other roads to peace may secure partial or temporary peace, but only God's peace surpasses human understanding to release us from inner turmoil. The peace exists. It exists for you and is offered to you. Take time to understand it and to find it.

6

The Threat to the Marriage

Ben and Jean quarreled about seventeen-year-old Nancy. Jean was suspicious. "Something's going on," she told Ben. "I think we ought to talk to her. She didn't come in until one last night."

Ben was reluctant to talk to Nancy. He felt his wife was being unnecessarily suspicious and that her suspicions would only deepen a rift which had begun to grow between daughter and parents. Ben's policy (if it could be called a policy) was to hope that the division was not serious and that it would heal itself with time. Jean on the other hand felt the rift called for action and that Ben was running away from the problem. So the two quarreled, and quarreled so fiercely that thirty minutes later Ben got a ticket for speeding on a highway close to their home.

Problems with children have as great a potential to strengthen marriage as to wreck it. They can bring you together in a new unity or blow you apart. Whatever rules or policies you have previously agreed on will be tested. And as rules and policies are tested, so likewise will your trust in each other. "The strain on our marriage has been tremendous," a missionary wrote me. Their problems with teen-age children brought the family back to the United States from a Central American country.

I cannot exaggerate the importance of parental harmony. Children need it and need it more than ever when they go wrong. Their well-being depends on it. The welfare of children rests more on parental unity than on any child-rearing expertise the parents may have. Parents can get away with many mistakes if their children see them as a solid, loving alliance. Such an alliance creates a context in which children can respond with respect and obedience.

Sometimes delinquency can be traced to a poor relationship between parents. The question then arises, How are healthy relations between spouses established and maintained?

Expecting Rights, Rejecting Responsibilities

Just as we saw was the case if you desire familial peace, if you are to live in marital harmony, you must have realistic expectations of one another. Bill feels disappointed and cheated because Mary will not sing duets in church with him. Mary dreads standing up in public. She has never had any interest in music. Bill on the other hand has a passable tenor voice and had always dreamed of singing duets with the woman of his choice. Such unrealistic expectations led to shouting from Bill, tears from Mary and insomnia for their three small children.

You may have based the expectations you had of your spouse on what you saw in your own parents (or on what you have read about ideal parenting) and assumed your partner shared corresponding ideals. In that case any harmony between you both rests on shaky ground.

Marriages commonly come to grief because of incompatible expectations about sex, money, religion, discipline of children and relationships with each other's friends and relatives. They are rocks on which many a marriage founders, rocks you should clearly mark on your marriage chart and around which you should plan a safely navigable passage. You can only do so, however, if you can both discuss your feelings openly and calmly. Happy is the couple who have done so before rebellious children have a chance to set the captains of the family vessel at each other's throats.

One would suppose that Christians have an advantage over others in that they are guided in marriage by Holy Scripture. Since the partners hold certain marriage ideals in common, there should logically be no need for discussion. The statistics do not seem to reflect any superiority of Christian marriages, however. Christian marriages break down over the same rocks as non-Christian marriages. While Christian divorces are less common, they may only be so because of the Christian taboo on divorce. A Christian couple may both subscribe to a common code, but unless they both view such a code as a guide to their responsibilities rather than to their rights, they will not find conjugal peace.

The Bible spells out the basics of the man/woman relationship in two well-known phrases: "Wives, be subject to your husbands, as to the Lord.... Husbands, love your wives, as Christ loved the church" (Eph. 5:22, 25). The phrases are unpopular in an age of equal rights. Rightly understood, biblical principles set optimal conditions for marital happiness, prescribing complementary attitudes in both partners. They suggest neither superiority in the man nor inferiority in the woman (such ideas are firmly dismissed in Gal. 3:28) but rather a mutuality or a complementarity of roles. Not only is the woman to submit to the man but the man to the woman (Eph. 5:21).

But the real problem lies not in the appropriateness of the demands made on each partner but in our human way of viewing those demands. The Bible focuses attention on responsibilities rather than on rights. A Christian husband may be concerned with his right to have a submissive wife. Having listened to sermons which misinterpret Paul's words and exhort him to secure his wife's submission in the marriage, he approaches marital problems with unnecessary belligerence or else is filled with resentment that he has been saddled with a "rebellious" wife. Christian wives fall prey to a similar error, being concerned more with their right to have a loving husband than with their own responsibilities.

In a good Christian marriage the concern of both partners with giving rather than with receiving love will make submission easier. Submission in turn will make love easier. Marriage has something in common with a trapeze act. There is grave risk in both, and neither seems inherently secure. Yet as each partner concentrates on performing his or her movements in the best way possible, a stunning, well-coordinated performance takes place. It is a performance both partners are proud of and satisfied with. But woe betide the trapeze artist whose preoccupation with a partner's performance leads to a deterioration in his or her own. Great will be somebody's fall!

Passive Father, Frustrated Mother, Rebellious Son
Problems among a passive father, a frustrated mother and a rebellious teen-ager are so common that they deserve special attention. By a passive father I mean one who generally avoids confrontation with his children and who may vacillate between forgetting about his responsibilities to discipline and care for them (his commoner reaction) and unnecessarily fierce onslaughts on them. Such a father may be articulate, successful at his job, outwardly cooperative with the counselor, capable of displaying incredible insight into his children's basic needs and yet inadequate in his role as husband and father.

As is so often the case, he is married to a woman who is emotionally warm, more suspicious of the children than her husband, probably overprotective and extremely frustrated because her husband fails to back her when she moves in to control difficult situations.

Mr. and Mrs. Gomez were such a couple. They came to see me about fourteen-year-old Adolfo, their son and third child. At our first interview Carlos, Maria and Adolfo were all present. In spite of my experience in family counseling I lost control of the interview at the very outset. For one and a half hours Carlos, a vice president of a large company, did nearly all the talking. He explained to me that in Argentina, where they had lived in a small city, Adolfo enjoyed many Christian friends. Only since coming to Canada had he fallen in with undesirable companions. Here in Canada there was no equivalent of the neighborhood social organizations such as existed in Argentina. The move had (according to Carlos) been more upsetting to Adolfo than to his daughters. The change, combined with difficulties in a new school system and an alien language, were, he felt, responsible for the change in Adolfo's behavior.

Throughout the interview Carlos spoke of "we" whenever he expressed his point of view. "It is our feeling. . . . We think. . . . We are quite certain. . . . " I presumed that he was speaking of Maria and himself though Maria gave no hint as to whether she agreed or disagreed with all he said.

My first attempts to draw Maria and Adolfo into the discussion were fruitless. Carlos always spoke for them telling me that Adolfo had been involved with drugs, that he didn't enjoy the company of the young people in their church, that he had been drunk on several occasions, that he had been caught shoplifting and that he stayed out late with undesirable companions—all in spite of the fact that he had once claimed to be a Christian. Carlos also told me that Maria was always "bugging the boy" and that some of his problems were due to Maria's being constantly "on the boy's back." I was a little irritated at the situation but could not dislike Carlos who seemed pleasant and anxious to get at the root of the problem.

Out of the corner of my eye I watched Adolfo, an under-sized boy with long black hair, high-heeled, highly polished boots and ragged jeans. He gave no sign of interest in his father's discourse but stared at the floor, sometimes contemplating his boots, sometimes chewing his nails. His father was tall and heavy, and his mother short and black haired like himself.

At one point toward the close of the interview Carlos was discussing Adolfo's defiance over the hour they set for him to return home each evening. Once during the evening meal he had forbidden him to go out that evening, "but he defied me."

"You mean he sneaked out when you weren't watching?"

"No," Maria spoke for almost the first time. "He told his father neither of us can stop him going out if he wants to go, but my husband said he would break Adolfo's back if he tried."

"And what happened?"

"Adolfo picked up the bread knife from the supper table," Maria said quietly, "and my husband let him go."

I turned to Carlos, "You let him get away with it?"

Gomez looked uncomfortable.

"What could I do?" he shrugged. "He would have used the knife. I don't believe in fighting physically with my son." Gomez was twice the size of his son. Suddenly I saw what I had begun to suspect: the self-possessed man who had so smoothly dominated the interview was a passive windbag. I addressed Adolfo.

"How did you feel when your dad backed down?"

At first the boy said nothing. Then he answered a single word. "Lousy."

"You mean you wanted your dad to make you stay in?"

"I don't know what I wanted. But I sure didn't want him to do *that*."

"To do what?"

"To act like he was afraid of me."

"That scared you more than if he had acted mad?"

"I dunno. At first it seemed great. . . . Yeah, it scared me. I felt sick. He couldn't make me do anything anymore." There was triumph neither in his voice nor in his eyes, only a look of mingled bewilderment and fear.

Carlos seemed to have shrunk. His self-possession had vanished. Maria began to pour out her concern for the boy. "Sure I bug him! Sure I get mad! But afterward we make friends and he says, 'I love you, mom.' But my husband does nothing. He doesn't even talk to him!"

It became even more clear in the next interview that the Carlos who was so self-possessed at work and in social situations was ineffective in the home. Maria, who had been silent for most of the interview, made the decisions and bullied and cajoled her children and husband into conforming to her wishes. But since both Maria and Adolfo needed a strong and competent husband and father, each was frustrated and driven to extremes of behavior that bothered both of them.

But there was a deeper cause to the conflict. Carlos and Maria were not united in their relationship with Adolfo. Maria vacillated between berating Adolfo and protecting him from her husband. Carlos incessantly criticized and resented his wife. The boy had driven them apart and now found himself caught between them. Because I was unable to help the parents communicate effectively, I was also unable to help solve Adolfo's problem. Still more serious, the weakness that may have led to Adolfo's problem seemed now to place the marriage itself in serious jeopardy as the new stress of Adolfo's behavior deepened their mutual resentment.

Ships in a Convoy

Seeking harmony between mates should have priority over most other goals for promoting familial harmony. The children need it as much as the marriage. And one helpful factor in true harmony is good communication. Although communication is a bit of a fad at present, it is still true that it contributes significantly to marital harmony.

Some experts on family counseling would say that all the causes of breakdown between spouses can be placed under that one heading. By *failure to communicate* they imply that neither parent tells the other how he or she feels about the children, what should be done about them, which parent should do what, what the basic problems are or what attitude each parent has to the other. Parents may feel they have communicated ("I *told* you that ages ago!" "But you know perfectly well how I feel." "You *did* know; you just don't want to admit it!") but the communication has not been effective. Each has been so absorbed by his or her views that neither has been listening to the other. Each mistakenly suspects the other of being negligent, unfeeling, willful or stubborn. Like ships in convoy that fail to follow the rules for keeping station, they tend either to drift apart or to collide.

Three kinds of communication breakdown between parents may occur in attempting to deal with children: a communication failure existing prior to problems with the child; a failure to share a common view of the problems concerning the child; and a failure to share a common view of the discipline that should be employed.

Pre-existing Communication Problems

Some parents lacked good communication before they ever ran into problems with their children, as in the case of Carlos and Maria. They may not have realized they were not communicating. They might have protested that their relationship was entirely satisfactory. But the problems existed nonetheless.

To communicate well in marriage you need two abilities. You must know how to listen accurately, sympathetically and with a determination to understand your spouse. In addition you must be free to express not only everyday information but your own feelings, attitudes and views. Both skills require practice. Most of us are more eager to speak than to listen. In many arguments the participants interrupt constantly, and in some casual conversations friends may in their eagerness talk simultaneously.

1. *Incoming communication: listening.* "Let every man be quick to hear, slow to speak," James cautions us (1:19). We speak because we want others to understand us and are impatient when they talk because we are quite sure we already understand them. Their excessive talking is unnecessary. We may go so far as to feel that they do not even understand themselves. They need to be set straight, to see issues as they ought to be seen. But our impatience is self-defeating. "A man convinced against his will is of the same opinion still." Unless people are sure they are being listened to sympathetically, they in turn will not listen.

We talk too much because we are too anxious. To listen to someone else's words drives us to a frenzy of impatience. We become irritated, upset. We must therefore curb our tongues. There is no need for fret or hurry for it does not matter that the other person is mistaken. It only matters that his or her concern be heeded, be listened to with patience and understanding.

To understand your wife does not necessarily mean to agree with her. It means to be silent as she speaks, to put yourself in her shoes, to listen closely to what she says, to watch her face and body for clues about how she feels, to say, "Could you say that again? I didn't understand exactly"; or, "I can see what you mean"; or, "You must have felt bad about that." It means to let the other person pick up the feeling that his or her concerns are indeed important to you, that you really do want to understand. Most of the time our desire is to be understood rather than to understand. But the most important part of communication is to listen well.

2. *Outgoing communication: speaking.* Paradoxically, in spite of the pressure with which words gush from our mouths, we may not be communicating when we do speak. Words can confuse. They can cover up. I do not mean that in our eagerness we lie but that our frenzy may spring from an unconscious need not to share the depths of our hearts. It is not easy to say to your spouse, "I was mad at you last night because you didn't come to bed when I asked." You may feel ashamed. You may even deny to yourself that last night's tiff has anything to do with this morning's argument. It is easier to criticize the way your spouse deals with the kids than to admit that you are pouting over something trivial.

You can only share a problem if you know what the problem is. Since most of us are so accustomed to fooling ourselves, we may lack the capacity even to see where the root of our distress lies. We need to pray with the psalmist, "Search me, O God, and know my heart! Try me and know my thoughts!" (Ps. 139:23). We deceive ourselves for fear of being shamed. How can we admit we are so childish, so neurotic? Worse, how can we expose ourselves to someone else? Even when our complaint is valid, how dare we risk defeat in a quarrel by mentioning it? Would it not be wise to avoid rocking the boat?

In many a marriage a host of petty resentments lie hidden since each of the partners has learned to forget them. But they may weaken the bonds of affection and commitment. Everything may appear to be in order but, like metal fatigue in machines and in bridges, the hidden resentments may only make their presence felt when new stresses are added and a breakdown surprises everybody.

My true feelings should not only be expressed but should be expressed helpfully. I must neither scream them nor mutter them into my beard. Let me not be afraid to look my spouse in the eye. Let me speak clearly and directly but without accusing. I must not say, "You never come to bed on time!" or, "You always promise to come to bed but you never do!" I must talk about myself and my feelings, not about my spouse's failures (real or supposed). It might be better to say (firmly, openly, clearly), "I feel ashamed to mention it but I was upset when you didn't come to bed last night. It's still bugging me." Your spouse may react defensively to what you say but not nearly so defensively as to an accusation. And if your spouse does reply defensively, you can say, "You may be right dear, but this is the way I feel."

To summarize, marital quarrels can be de-escalated by following certain basic rules:

1. Pay more attention to understanding than to being understood, to listening rather than speaking. Be interested in the other's point of view.

2. Learn to recognize why you are feeling upset.

3. Learn to express your feelings clearly, simply and not accusingly.

Agreement on the Problem
It is never easy to know in its beginning whether disturbing behavior is a phase or a harbinger of serious trouble. "He wanted to think it was a phase," one mother wrote me, "and I felt differently about the changes in our son. I saw the real ... problem, and he wanted to ignore it. I feel mothers *sense* things because they feel whereas men think. My husband is a thinker and seldom shows any feeling. One has to be really emotionally upset before he responds."

The problem in this case was not merely one of two people seeing the same son differently but of the mother experiencing apprehension and the father not. Perhaps it didn't matter who was right. As events turned out the mother's fears not the father's complacency were justified. There would have been more harmony and less anxiety had the conversation gone like this:

Father   This is worrying you, isn't it?

Mother   It is worrying me. It's worrying me a great deal.

Father   What d'you think we should do about it?
Mother   I don't know. I stay awake at night worrying myself sick. . . .
Father   Should we talk to him about it?

For in such a case spouses should not merely be looking at the problem child but at each other's fears and anxieties. These must not be brushed under the carpet but dealt with promptly and openly.

Clearly parents should agree on issues like privileges, discipline, tidiness, time spent with parents, table manners, homework and a host of practical matters. If there is no agreement, that is to say if each feels critical of the way the other handles the children, disagreements in this area must be thrashed out thoroughly, preferably not in the presence of the children.

Nothing is more destructive to the whole family than to have two parents with conflicting sets of rules and policies. Children quickly pick up the differences and play one parent against the other.

You are almost certain to disagree with your spouse on some issues. Both of you arrived at your present opinions after being exposed to your respective parents' methods, to books and articles on child rearing and to sermons on the Bible's view of discipline. Since you did not share the same parents, may not always have read the same literature and may have listened to different preachers who interpret Scripture in different ways, it is likely that points of difference will arise.

If you have a habit of arguing in front of the children, discuss the matter with your partner. You may not be able to stop right away. Therefore you should think of ways to prevent the arguments either from getting out of hand or from affecting the relationship between parents and children.

The most difficult occasion is the one where you disagree strongly about a request calling for immediate action.

Son   May I stay over at Peter's tonight?
Mother   Yes, I think so. I don't see why not.
Father   Oh, but I do! He's got that physics assignment that was going to take him all night to complete. . . .
Son   But dad, Peter's doing the assignment too. We're going to work on it together. If I go right now I'll just have time to catch the bus.
Mother   No, you don't have to do that, dear. I'll drive you. I have to stop by the Smiths' anyway. Just let me comb my hair.
Father   Now look here. . . .

At this point the ball is in father's court. I believe that no single correct solution exists for him. If he still disagrees and is sure his judgment will be accepted, he might find it easy to say, "No, son. I'm afraid I can't let you go tonight. You really ought to have let us know before this. You'll have to postpone your visit to Peter. Tonight you're going to have to stay home and work on your physics assignment. If you need help, I'll be glad to give you a hand." On the other hand if father guesses that such a remark would lead to a more prolonged and a possibly emotion-charged argument with his wife, he could equally well say, "Oh, all right then. I'm not sure that I like the idea, but perhaps you and I can talk about it later, dear."

In the first instance the family would play it father's way, and in the second, mother's.

The important point is not who wins the argument, nor even whether the best decision was made about the visit to Peter, but that a parental rift not open in front of the son. It is better to concede victory to your spouse under such circumstances, even to go along with a decision which is against your better judgment, than to expose him to parental disunity. In the battle for family stability, you will have sacrificed a pawn to take a bishop.

Clearly some arguments are harmless and can happily be conducted in the presence of and along with the children. But where the argument grows destructive, it is good to have a prearranged "self-destruct" mechanism. There could, for instance, be a code phrase which both parents recognize, something like, "O.K. How about if we play it your way for now? Maybe we could discuss it more thoroughly when we have more time." If both of you should be irritated, you may find it hard to stop in midargument, swallow and cooly pronounce the code phrase. But it might be worth it.

However, it is important to realize that the system will never work unless you trust each other and are both genuinely willing to concede points for the benefit of an ongoing alliance. It is true unity that you need, not the superficial appearance of unity. Don't be a silent critic either. Ask your spouse whether he or she has considered alternate ways of handling things. Some parents are unable to agree. But it is not necessary to see eye to eye with your spouse on every issue. On minor things we may differ or make compromises. Do not insist that everyone in the family agree with you or admit you are right. On the other hand do not hide your disagreement from each other, especially if the issues are important to you. Hidden issues are the ones that cause us to fly into an unexpected rage, without knowing why. So learn to spot such issues and share them helpfully.

Here then is a fourth guideline for communication:

4. If your partner cannot see your point and if disagreement remains, agree to differ. Never pretend there is agreement when there is not, and do not insist on resolving every disagreement.

Agreement on the Discipline

Parents should have a common front before the children and be utterly loyal to each other. When Danny asks, "May I go outside, dad?" dad should reply, "I don't see why not, but did you check whether your mother wants anything?" And if mother has already refused to grant permission he might add, "Danny, you ought to know better than to come to me when your mother has already said no. Your mother and I stick together, you know."

Ideally you will continually update and modify your policies, adapting them to changing circumstances in the light of experience. In the course of time you will discover that while your spouse may seem to have certain weaknesses, he or she may also display valuable strengths which you will grow to appreciate. You may find that each of you is strong in an area where the other is weak, that you complement each other and make a good working team.

I had always felt that my wife Lorrie was too suspicious of the children and was too inclined to scold. She, on the other hand, mistrusted certain policies I felt to be essential. We discussed our views about the children often and at length. As time went on each of us developed profound respect for the other's abilities. I discovered Lorrie's suspicions proved correct too frequently to be taken lightly, and she was impressed by the fruits of some of my long-range policies. From being uneasy partners in child rearing we became a close working team. At one point we had fears that problems with one of our children might be driving us apart. But the free communication between us produced the opposite effect: we were drawn together by those very problems.

Commonly the wife complains that she is left with the lion's share of the discipline, but occasionally I run across husbands who complain that their wives undermine discipline. The problem usually is compounded by differing ideas about what *ought* to be done. Occasionally, however, parents agree about what ought to be done, but not about who should do it.

Again problems must be brought into the open and thrashed out. If no solution is apparent it is good to find a counselor both parents can trust. Dad may have difficulty facing the task of discipline. He may shrink from the unpleasantness and may fear the loss of his children's love. "I don't see why I have to be the ogre," parents often tell me.

Nobody likes to be an ogre. All of us want our children's love. Yet we need to face our fears, to talk about them and to conquer them. Children do not love parents they can control. They despise them. Love cannot exist without respect.

If your marriage is intact, then under most circumstances it is better for both of you to be present when you cross-examine your children or when you discipline them. If you find yourself shrinking from a joint interview, ask yourself why. Your reluctance could be a sign that you are lacking unity with your spouse or that your own relationship with one of the children is on a different footing than that of your spouse. In either case it is important that the differences or the lack of unity be remedied. Remember, your relationship with your spouse should be primary.

One of you can act as spokesman if you prefer it, but the nonspokesman should make it clear that he or she is a full partner in what is going on. You may sometimes try to reach a common agreement before meeting with the son or daughter in question. A full discussion of the issues beforehand may prevent confusion when you deal with the child.

On the other hand you cannot afford to be too rigid, or to make final decisions before you both know all the facts. Your agreement should be about principles (rather than about details), which should serve to promote a working unity between you. New information arising when you talk with your children may call for a modification of your previous view. In this case one spouse might say to the other, "Well, what Terry tells us may mean we should reconsider what we had decided. Perhaps we should tell him no. . . . "

If it is impossible or, for some special reason, undesirable that you interview together, then the absent parent must be kept accurately informed. And if you are the absent party, you should, remembering that decisions are not easy to make, support those your spouse has made.

If you feel that they are unacceptable and both of you can

subsequently come to an agreement in the matter, then changes should be made in such a manner as not to undermine the authority of either parent. Suppose, for example, that mom feels dad has been too severe with Phyllis in sentencing her to be grounded for a week when she came home half an hour late. If both parents arrive at an agreement in the matter, then dad can go to Phyllis and say, "I've been talking to your mother about your coming home late. She thinks I was too severe in grounding you for so long. I've thought some more about it, and I'm inclined to agree with her. So we'll change the punishment. . . . " Dad's authority will not be undermined provided mother remains loyal to him and refuses the role of perpetual mediator.

Sharing Family Plans and Prayers
Some matters should be treated with the strictest confidence. If David with great embarrassment and shame approaches his parents with a confession of an offense which affected none of his brothers and sisters, then it will be a shameful breach of trust for his parents to reveal the matter to the rest of the family. Similarly there are plans which should be kept secret, either because a breach of confidence would be involved in revealing them or because a happy surprise is planned.

But there are some sins and weaknesses and some projects and plans which unite the family. Wise parents will know the difference between what should and what should not be shared. If the family has a regular prayer time, then a sense of unity can be an important spin-off when such items are prayed about together. Questions can be asked and suggestions invited. Burdens of individuals become burdens the whole family gets under. Even quarrels and differences can be lovingly prayed over.

Prayer is what brings heavenly powers to operate within the home. Its psychological benefits are only secondary. Nevertheless they are real and many healings have begun where familial and marital wounds were the subject of family prayer.

Let me summarize two last communication ground rules:

5. Both parents should agree on discipline to be taken and be present under normal circumstances when you are dealing with one of the children.

6. A family prayer time where some basic family issues or plans are exposed can contribute to healthy family relationships.

I began this chapter by warning that problems with children can drive parents apart. I have also said that the opposite can happen: the new stresses, even though they might show weakness, may by so doing cause both partners to build a better and firmer marriage. It can go either way. What may seem hopeless tragedy often becomes unbelievable blessing.

I have given up trying to predict what will happen in marriages where there are problems with the children. Some situations have seemed hopeless. Yet none is. If both parents agree that, by whatever measures, the marriage must remain intact and be strengthened and if both put confidence in God (the inventor of marriage), no situation can be labeled hopeless.

7
Professional Help

When should a parent seek professional help for a daughter or son who creates problems? How can a parent decide what sort of help is needed and who is best qualified to give it? What dangers lurk inside the offices of psychologists, social workers, psychiatrists and counselors? Will they widen the split between my child and me? Will they criticize me? Subtly belittle me? Show up my ignorance? Undermine my faith?

Should a Christian ever seek help from a non-Christian? Don't the Scriptures contain all the wisdom I need? Do ungodly professionals have more on the ball than the Holy Spirit? Isn't it really compromising (sort of "going down to Egypt") to consult a professional? Will I be showing lack of faith by doing so?

Help for What?
Let us be clear what we are asking. What do we need? Obviously one doesn't ask a plumber for advice on gardening or a musician to diagnose cancer. Nor would one normally consult a pastor about the color scheme in the living room or a

Sunday-school teacher about an investment portfolio.

Matters may not be so clear of course. If God is an expert on everything, presumably we should need no help from other experts. But God is not a substitute encyclopedia. Who looks to God for information the yellow pages were designed to give? Who prays for directions to find Brown Street when there is a city map in the glove compartment? Who, for that matter, prays for their thirst to be quenched when a faucet lies at hand? Why seek from God a cure for weariness when a bed is waiting and the hour to get into it has arrived? God is not a Celestial Convenience. He has provided us with normal means, and in our relationship with him we shall make little progress if we fail to use them.

But God and the Scriptures deal with moral and spiritual issues. How can we consult a psychologist if the problem is basically one of righteousness and faith? Will not the psychologist smile condescendingly and tell us there is no problem?

One father said to me, "Unless the person is a believer I wouldn't welcome help from professionals. I have a psychologist in a prayer group, and I have observed other psychologists and psychiatrists. They have problems they are seeking answers for, so why should I seek their help?"

Another wrote, "Any help should be from Christians who are obeying the Lord Jesus Christ and using the Word of God prayerfully. 'Without me ye can do nothing.' Why seek the counsel of the ungodly?"

Yet another wrote, "I had a bad experience with a social worker living as a guest in my own home. He was not very qualified to help." But he continued ambivalently, "For some strange reason neither my wife nor I sought help for ourselves or our child. We perhaps should have done so. Maybe we wanted to cover up our 'less than perfection.' Perhaps we did not want to face the fact of problems in the family. I personally am very wary of psychiatrists and social workers. Sometimes they can have some very 'kooky' ideas."

One mother told me about her widely differing experiences with professionals. "The first doctor did not help me at all. I felt very disappointed and at a deep loss. It was a waste of time. I lost hope. . . . Yes, I do feel the need for help and am at present getting just that, even though my first experience was a bad one."

Another parent wrote, "I had professional help from Dr. C. [a Christian psychologist]. . . . He helped me terrifically in many areas to understand myself, to not feed hostility but to starve it, no matter how hard it is." This parent continued to praise her psychologist for almost a page of close typing.

Obviously professionals vary, not only in their faith but in their capacity to help. Some are warm others cold. Some are wise and experienced, others green and silly. Some are so tied to theory that they view all problems through the spectacles of their ideological prejudices. Others hold theories lightly because they are keenly aware that problems and people do not always fit into little boxes. Some are pompous and conceited, others gentle and compassionate. In short, they are human beings.

Even in matters of faith there is no black and white. There are crooked, incompetent Christians whose primary interest is making a fast buck or in playing the big shot. There are competent, courteous non-Christians who, though they may know less about the Scriptures than you do, will from their wide experience be able to offer solid help in areas you have never thought about.

Experts in counseling are no different from experts in any other area. They are technicians, technicians in human behavior, perhaps even in brain mechanisms and bodily functions. We all know stealing is wrong, but sometimes experts can put their finger on the reason that stealing is a special temptation to Herman. In the same way, we all know that children should not dodge homework. But psychologists can sometimes identify special difficulties Carol has with symbols, the reason for her distractability.

Most phenomena can be explained in different ways. You are sitting, let us say, in your living room listening to a record on the stereo and a visitor from outer space asks, "Why is the room filled with strange sounds?"

We could give our visitor at least two varieties of explanation. One kind would have to do with recording techniques, musical instruments, woofers and tweeters. It would be a technical explanation concerning the reproduction of sound. On the other hand we could say, "The room is filled with strange sounds because I felt lonely and wanted to be comforted. The sounds are what we call music." This would be a more teleological explanation, or if you prefer to view the matter another way, a psychological explanation. Notice that both explanations have to do with cause, one with immediate causes and the other with ultimate causes. They are entirely different explanations, yet they are neither contradictory nor mutually exclusive. Each corresponds to a different meaning of the word *why*. In the same way, human behavior can be explained by different types of explanation which are in no way contradictory.

I once talked to a sixteen-year-old boy who had killed several police officers in a shoot-out round his home. Why had he shot them? Killing is evil, and we may rightly say that his actions were immoral. He killed because of murderous fear and hate. Yet as I talked to him I saw another side to the matter. "Why did you shoot the police?"

"They weren't police. They were just disguised as police."

"What makes you say that?"

"Because their eyes were blue—vivid blue—shining right at me."

"I don't understand what you mean."

"They are from outer space. They are going to destroy the world. . . . "

Clearly there was another aspect to the killing. Because his mind was deranged, my patient was in the grip of delusional terror. A couple of weeks later, responding to appropriate medication, he was appalled by the horror of his own actions. Had he received proper technical help at an earlier state the tragedy would never have occurred.

Christian parents may see only the *moral* aspect of a problem. Professionals, while not ignoring the moral aspect, can identify the psychological aspect which may or may not be of importance. In the case of some of my patients it can be of very great importance.

Nicki, age sixteen, was subject to bursts of rage at school and at home. He talked incessantly, laughed hilariously at times, slept only four hours every night, was overactive and got into fist fights constantly. Seen by a psychiatrist who specialized in problems of adolescence, he was diagnosed as hypomanic. On a small dose of lithium carbonate (an inert salt) his excessive talking and activity were reduced to normal, and his rages, his inappropriate laughter and fighting all disappeared. Rages and fighting have moral, psychological and physical aspects. Nicki's psychiatrist detected a psychological disturbance underlying the outbursts. Once this was regulated, Nicki's temptation to give way to fighting and bursts of rage was dramatically reduced.

Once the nearest help (other family members, teachers, pastors) has failed the parents, they commonly turn to counselors, social workers, psychiatrists and psychologists. How can they know which to turn to first? How much difference does it make if the professional is a Christian? Usually parents want counsel for themselves or for their children. Sometimes they hope, unrealistically, that the professional will make the problem disappear. But matters are rarely so simple as in the case of Nicki.

Sometimes the psychological aspect of the problem is insignificant. Sometimes a rebellious will or an unbelieving heart are a sufficient explanation of behavior that troubles an anxious parent. Or sometimes a psychological reason exists that lies beyond the powers of science to solve. For our science is crude and feeble and it has to be confessed that whether for our want of knowledge or because of the rebellious bent in the mind of many a child, those youngsters helped by the human technicians still form a minority of those who seek help.

What help then can parents expect from a counselor? Experienced counselors can draw from personal knowledge of problems to attempt to answer two questions: first, what is the underlying cause of the problem, and second, how serious is it? They might also be able to give parents an idea of how the problem can be helped and what the future is likely to bring.

If they are honest, they may have to admit that they do not know what the underlying cause is or that they have no help to offer. To the best of their knowledge the outlook is very gloomy. Or they may be able to refer the parents to another professional who has special skills.

Common Problems Requiring Professional Help
Let us first look at one or two serious problems in teen-agers that call for professional help and then, having done so, discuss varieties of counselors and their usefulness.

1. *Pregnancy.* Few things shake parents so much as pregnancy in a teen-age daughter. Most parents assume that an illegitimate pregnancy is something that only happens in other families.

A pregnant girl, fearful of a strong reaction from her parents, may already have sought an abortion. Since abortions legal or illegal cost money and since in most areas where abortions are permitted parental consent is needed for minors, parents may have the double shock of learning that their daughter is seeking an abortion for a pregnancy they knew nothing about. More commonly the girl is too confused to take any definite line of action and may disguise her condition as long as possible, not allowing herself to face the inevitability of a dénouement and the need to make serious decisions. Sometimes such a girl will run away. Or she might confide in her parents at an early stage. Sometimes friends, a schoolteacher or a school counselor may be the ones through whom the parents learn what has happened.

A number of options face the girl and her parents. The pregnancy can be interrupted. It may be allowed to go to term and the baby be adopted at birth through an agency. It may, on the other hand, be adopted by the girl's own parents, or she may keep the baby herself. Finally, the father of the child may marry the girl, in which case the couple could generally keep the baby.

Abortion is a measure that Christians would normally oppose, some feeling that it can never be justified, others that it is justifiable only in certain limited circumstances. Physicians may recommend it if the life of the mother is threatened or if her physical or emotional health is seriously in jeopardy. Thus it may be justified in very young girls or when a pregnancy results from criminal rape. Recently in my area a twelve-year-old girl who had been raped by a violent sex offender was granted a therapeutic abortion on the grounds of her emotional health.

Whatever view you may hold about the morality of abortion, you should think carefully before recommending the measure to your daughter. It is true that a girl in her early teens is not equipped emotionally to be a mother, and it is also true that some young girls are damaged emotionally by carrying the baby to term. However, abortion itself can leave emotional scars. Some studies indicate that the chances of emotional damage from an abortion are greater than from bringing the baby to term.

By assessing your daughter's emotional health carefully, experienced adolescent psychiatrists or psychologists may be of help should such a question arise. They will probably not give advice either for or against abortion. That decision must be made by you, your daughter and in many areas by a special hospital committee. But they can give you an idea of the emotional consequences to your daughter. Having examined her they will have some idea of her emotional make-up. Having access to studies on the effects of abortions on young mothers and of the baby being taken away for adoption, they may be able to predict what would happen to her in either eventuality. Pro-life organizations exist in most cities now and are eager to give emotional support and counsel to those who are distressed by pregnancy and need help in sorting out the issues. Yet here too one needs to realize certain biases may be present in the help offered.

If your daughter is pregnant, be very careful about the question of adoption. An older girl, able to care for herself, may rightly claim that the decision to keep the baby or to have it adopted is hers. But if she works to earn her living or is a full-time student, who will take care of the baby? Most middle-aged mothers of teen-age daughters shrink at the realization that the chief responsibility for the child will fall on them and not on the baby's mother.

The implications both of keeping the baby and of allowing it to be adopted should be discussed fully and frankly by everyone concerned. Finally, whatever decision is reached must not be made *for* the pregnant daughter. Though the temptation to take command will be great, especially because of the tendency to overcompensate for failure to keep your daughter out of trouble, you must resist it. The decision needs to be made *with* her and *by* her.

2. *Alcoholism.* You should suspect your son or daughter has a major alcohol problem if he or she has been drunk on several occasions over a period of a year or more. Definitions of alcoholism are unsatisfactory. Perhaps the best and simplest is that alcoholics are those who have lost control of their drinking and who by drinking are damaging themselves socially,

physically or otherwise. Thus if your child's drinking has been associated with delinquent behavior on several occasions, you should suspect alcoholism.

Face your son or daughter with the possibility that he or she has an alcohol problem. Make it quite clear that an alcoholic is not someone who is down and out but simply someone who gets into trouble with drinking. Make it clear, too, that there is nothing you, the parent, can do to solve the problem. The only solution is for him or her to renounce alcohol for life. Otherwise it may slowly gain complete mastery in his or her life.

You may not be sure of the seriousness of the problem. Most social workers, psychologists, psychiatrists and counselors are competent to assess and give an opinion on the matter.

It is better not to paint drinking alcohol as a grave sin, partly because drinking, unlike drunkenness, is not in itself a sin and partly because unresolved feelings of guilt add to the problem of drinking rather than help solve it. As a rule of thumb we could say that the guiltier alcoholics feel, the more likely they are to drink.

It makes good sense, then, to focus on the folly rather than on the sin of drinking. The sense of guilt is already paralyzingly present. The thought that drinking is "crazy", "dumb" or "stupid" (because of the trouble it creates for the person who drinks) can on the other hand open up a new and helpful perspective. "Sinful? Yes, it's sinful," you can say, "but it's also pretty dumb. . . . " Not only should you point out the folly without disparaging your child's personality, but you should also not protect your child from the consequences of the folly, on the contrary let him or her face them squarely.

Psychotherapy and counseling have almost universally proved unavailing for alcoholism. Most experienced therapists would agree that while it may or may not be true that certain psychological problems underlie alcoholism, it proves futile in practice to try to solve those problems until the alcoholic has stopped drinking.

Some behaviorists have demonstrated in carefully controlled studies that alcoholics can learn controlled drinking and that such a goal is more likely to achieve success than the goal of total abstinence. Unfortunately, the follow-up studies, while impressive, rarely continue for more than six months so that no one knows what happens eventually to the "controlled" drinkers. In any case no studies of this type that I know of have been carried out on young people. It would be wiser in their case to hold up the goal of total abstinence.

Institutions exist all over North America with residential treatment for alcoholics varying from two weeks to several months in duration. A few institutions have a Christian orientation. The expense and the value of treatment programs vary widely. It is wise to find out all you can about any institution before you suggest that your teen-ager avail him or herself of the treatment. AA (Alcoholics Anonymous) groups are usually not suitable for adolescents who feel out of place among older men and women. Alateens sometimes is helpful for them, even though its aim is to help adolescents cope with drinking parents.

You will notice that I said *suggest.* My reason for doing so is that universal experience has demonstrated that someone with an alcohol problem must *want* help before help can be effective.

Temporary respite from the problem of drinking can be gained through administering Antabuse (disulfiram), a drug which can be taken orally. After one or two days of medication, drinking alcohol makes drinkers feel unwell, experience skin flushing, palpitations, headaches and perhaps nausea and vomiting. The knowledge that this will happen is sufficient to keep them from the temptation to drink. It becomes in effect a talisman protecting the drinker from sudden enticement.

Albert, age sixteen, had a serious drinking problem. He agreed that it was a problem and said he was willing to accept help. His father, after speaking with the family physician, explained the purpose of Antabuse and made the stipulation that if Albert were to be allowed to live at home, he must take a daily dose of the drug. The dose would be prescribed by their physician and administered daily by Albert's father.

During his first week on Antabuse, Albert made two attempts to test out the effectiveness of the medication. He took only a couple of sips of wine each time but felt sufficiently unwell to recognize that the medication was working. Since that time he has dropped the friends with whom he drank and is much more settled at home.

Don't expect miracles from Antabuse. It can only give a temporary respite until your son or daughter can come to terms with the problem. It is useless as a lifelong protection. Once Albert leaves home he can stop taking Antabuse any time he is tempted to drink. Within forty-eight hours he will be safe from the effects of the drug if he starts drinking again. So long as he remains at home his parents, with Albert's compliance, are controlling his drinking. The real goal should be that Albert control his drinking himself because he himself is convinced of the importance of doing so.

Conversion to Christ may be a help with the problem. The sense of cleansing, the new start, the vision of Christ—all are powerful factors pulling your son or daughter away from the problem. But conversion does not automatically solve the problem. One would suppose that it must, but experience demonstrates the contrary. Excessive drinking can have the same hold on a Christian as any other "besetting sin."

Finally, realize that you cannot (except with Antabuse and under the circumstances I described) prevent your child from getting into a mess by drinking. Sternness, discipline and punishment almost always prove ineffective. The solution is in your child's hands. Accept the fact that *you* cannot solve your child's alcohol problem—not only for your child's sake but for your own sanity.

3. *Homosexuality.* To discover your child is involved in homosexual practices will come as a terrible jolt. (Understatement.) But hold steady. If you are to help your child, panic and rage should be allowed to subside before you talk.

The seriousness of the situation will vary with age and with how extensive and long-standing the homosexual practices have been. A fourteen-year-old who has dabbled once or twice with erotic play is not in so deep as a seventeen-year-old who has been engaged for months with a serious homosexual affair. I have written about the problem of homosexuality in *Eros Defiled.*[1] Here I would like to make only one or two comments.

Your child may or may not want help. He or she may not even want to discuss the issue. If this is the case, there is little you can do. The longer the practice has continued, the less likely it is that your child will want to quit. Some homosexuals can be helped to reorient their homosexuality if they desire help. With others the reorientation is extremely difficult. For many Christian homosexuals the only solution is sexual abstinence. If your child is willing, it may be helpful to consult an experienced psychiatrist or psychologist.

If you want to get a glimpse of the inside of the mind of a homosexual, I suggest you read Alex Davidson's *The Returns of Love,*[2] a sensitive and moving account of the struggles of one Christian homosexual.

4. *Mental illness.* Almost inevitably when a child's behavior is bizarre and inexplicable, parents will turn anxiously to a psychiatrist. Dreaded terms like insanity, nervous breakdown, schizophrenia begin to suggest themselves.

Mental illness poses at least three kinds of problems for Christian parents. The first concerns the future. As frightening changes take place in the way their child thinks, talks, behaves, and as the child they once knew and loved turns into a stranger, they begin to ask, "What does the future hold? How will this end? Will our child ever be able to earn a living? Be independent?"

Then come questions concerning their relationship with the child. "Are we making our child worse by our attitudes? How should we behave?"

Deeper questions plague other parents. "What is mental illness? Does it really exist? Or is it (as some writers, both Christian and non-Christian confirm) merely a myth? Is it the result of sin? And if so, is the sin mine or my child's? Worse yet, is the condition a manifestation of demon possession?"

The scope of such questions is too broad, and the issues raised by them too complex to be discussed adequately here. However, let me say a word about the third group of questions. Mental illness does exist. The strange behavior that accompanies it is often associated with changes in body and brain, changes that can to some extent be corrected by medication. Since the 1950s certain chemical substances have changed the face of psychiatry. They are variously referred to as neuroleprics or as psychotropics. They fall into two broad classes: mood-modifying drugs and antipsychotic drugs.

They are important not only because of their power to modify the form of mental illness—which has made it possible to treat many such illnesses outside of a hospital—but because they have opened up the way to new research in neurochemistry, to a new understanding of brain and nerve mechanisms.

The medications we have are relatively crude instruments and our understanding of neurochemistry is still primitive. We must also beware of thinking of human behavior only in terms of biology. Biology and psychology are two sides of one coin, and it is equally important that we understand both. Nevertheless, dramatic strides in neurochemistry have been made. While we have a long way to go, the outlook for those with mental illness is much better than it was even thirty years ago.

The medications I speak of are neither unpleasant to take nor habit-forming. They are not a substitute for counseling, nor should mentally ill persons be relieved of the demand to act responsibly or to think rationally. Properly used, psychotropic drugs, by normalizing the operation and integration of the central nervous system, make it easier for sufferers to distinguish between reality and fantasy, and to assess their own problems realistically.

Mental illness is no more and no less related to sin and to demonic activity than are cancer, diabetes, or pneumonia. Some illnesses are the direct result of sin. Injuries from car accidents may result from drunken driving, and brain syphilis from sexual promiscuity. More commonly the relation is indirect. We are vulnerable to sickness (mental and physical) because we are fallen sons and daughters of a fallen Adam and Eve. It is just as appropriate to seek medical help for psychiatric illness as it is to do so for asthma or rheumatism or ulcers.

Clinical psychologists and psychiatrists have the best understanding of mental illness and are the source of the most reliable help in individual cases. Like experts in all fields they may make mistakes, whether in diagnosing the conditions or in answering questions about them. But there is no better human help available. Local Christian physicians and pastors may be in the best position to channel parents to the most appropriate help in the area.

Types of Counselors
The term *counselor* is gradually becoming an umbrella term covering everything from those who give intensive psychotherapy to others who offer gentle advice. Some are referred to as counselors though they never chose the title and do not particularly want it.

Thus social workers, nurses, psychiatrists, psychologists, welfare workers, school guidance counselors and a host of other professionals who are consulted about personal problems have come to be known as counselors. Training courses in counseling are multiplying and graduates may be referred to as pastoral counselors, marriage counselors or family counselors, according to the nature of the training they have received.

Because the training of counselors varies widely their skills will likewise vary, some having special skills that others lack. Psychiatrists and psychologists, for example, will have a better working knowledge of the central nervous system than say pastoral counselors whose expertise lies in biblical and doctrinal knowledge. Even more important as I indicated earlier, the experience, the personalities and the attitudes of counselors vary to affect their usefulness.

There are thus two kinds of information one should seek about counselors: first, about their training and theoretical orientation and second, about their personality. Both kinds of information are important, and if one kind is more important than the other, I would say (though many professional colleagues would disagree with me) that it is their personalities, their length of experience, their degree of interest in each client, their capacity for warmth, their objectivity and freedom from prejudice. As to the different kinds of counselors and the training they receive, sketches of some of them follow below.

1. *Pastors.* Some pastors give time to counseling even though they have had no special training. Others take special courses from seminaries or from seminaries in conjunction with university behavioral science departments. Their training may include a theoretical review of different psychological schools along with some practical supervision of clients they counsel during their training. It may lead to a doctoral degree and even postdoctoral work. Usually the training places special emphasis on marital and premarital counseling. Some pastoral counselors are trained to administer psychological

tests to people they seek to help.

2. *Psychologists.* Psychologists are specialists in human behavior whose primary interest is in normal rather than abnormal behavior. Many psychologists devote themselves to research, studying animals to gain clues about human behavior or else studying undergraduates, the species of human they have the greatest access to. They could be referred to as *non-clinical* psychologists.

Other psychologists are trained to administer tests, tests that attempt to evaluate personality, intelligence and potential problem areas. Increasing numbers of psychologists are interested in counseling which they may refer to as psychotherapy. (The term *psychotherapy* was originally coined by psychoanalysts to refer to a modified form of psychoanalysis. Nowadays *psychotherapy* can mean whatever the user of the term wants it to mean and is often used synonymously with counseling.)

Psychologists who administer tests and those who give counsel both refer to themselves as *clinical* psychologists. Their theoretical orientations may vary widely. I meet psychologists whose views are psychoanalytic, others who are followers of Piaget, others who are essentially humanists, still others who adhere to one of the many behaviorist schools and some who are interested in gestalt psychology, to mention only a few. Christian psychologists who have thought carefully about psychological theories in relation to a biblical view of human nature are in a position to make use of the insights from various schools without adopting the underlying philosophies associated with them.

Clinical psychologists differ also according to the ages of the clients who interest them. Thus there are child psychologists, adolescent psychologists and so on. Or again, psychologists may take a special interest in group psychotherapy, in family therapy or in T groups.

3. *Psychiatrists.* Psychiatrists are physicians who have

specialized in mental illness. Unlike psychologists they have a greater tendency to focus on abnormal rather than normal behavior. As a psychiatrist myself, I believe our greatest usefulness lies in the diagnosis and the treatment of the graver forms of emotional disturbance. However, psychiatrists vary as much in interests, activities and beliefs as do psychologists. In many medical schools and universities psychologists and psychiatrists work together in departments of human behavior.

Perhaps the most significant difference between the two is that in most areas in the Western Hemisphere only psychiatrists, because they are physicians, are permitted to prescribe medication. It is possible that economic and political factors will gradually force psychiatrists back into the role of medical consultants, but at present many psychiatrists prefer to spend a great deal of their time giving psychotherapy or counseling.

While all psychiatrists are physicians specializing in mental illness, psychoanalysts are psychiatrists who have undergone psychoanalysis themselves and have taken training from a recognized training analyst. (Psychoanalysis is a school of thought which originated with Sigmund Freud and which now has many forms.) Outside North America one may practice as a psychoanalyst without being a physician since psychoanalysis does not involve administering medication.

4. *Social workers.* Psychologists, psychiatrists, education and pastoral counselors may all be engaged in giving counsel of varying kinds and depths, sometimes referring to the counsel as psychotherapy. Social workers, too, whose role used to be conceived as that of giving direction to people whose distress called for social help, are now increasingly engaged in general and marital counseling and psychotherapy. Their training may include both theoretical and clinical exposure to psychological theories and to counseling practice.

5. *Nonprofessional groups.* It should be clear by now that while I have a healthy regard for good training and proper qualifications I have an even greater respect for experience,

intuitive perceptiveness and a capacity for warmth. This being the case I would not hesitate at times to recommend the help of nonprofessional agencies. It is impossible in a short book of this kind to give comprehensive and accurate information on the many nonprofessional groups that exist, and it would be best to limit myself to the most widely known—Alcoholics Anonymous.

AA rose out of the Oxford Group Movement (now known as Moral Rearmament). Its history and philosophy are set out in what is known as *The Black Book*. It is not Christian. Its members look for help not from God as he is but from whatever idea of God makes sense to them. I cannot therefore recommend the theological stance of AA, but I must pay tribute to the work it has done in helping alcoholics stay dry. The group support, the insistence on absolute honesty with oneself and others, the relentless challenging of dishonesty and self-pity—all are positive and helpful and are emphases a Christian can heartily support. It is a profound pity that such support and such honesty are not present in many local churches which are hopelessly inept in handling alcoholics.

Two sister organizations follow similar traditions: Alanon and Alateens. Alanon is an organization of spouses of alcoholics and Alateens is one of children of alcoholics. In many ways their work is more valuable than that of AA. By teaching spouses and children of alcoholics how to behave toward them (stressing especially the importance of allowing alcoholics to experience the consequences of their actions), Alateens and Alanon help keep families together and force alcoholics to face their problem and get help.

6. *School guidance centers.* Sometimes help is offered to children via school systems. Many school systems enjoy the resources of child guidance centers staffed by social workers, psychologists, speech therapists, education specialists and psychiatrists. Once teachers see that a child has problems, especially ones that guidance counselors in the school are

unable to handle, the school may request (with or without the parents' knowledge and consent) help from the guidance center.

In most cases the system is beneficial and works for the child's good. Almost invariably the guidance center will contact parents who will be interviewed by a member of the center's staff in order to get more information about the child's problem.

Christian parents are sometimes uneasy about the kind of help the center offers, help which may range from speech therapy to psychoanalytic psychotherapy. They face a choice between accepting what the center has to offer (usually without any charge) and opting for private help for which they will have to pay.

It is hard for me to give guidelines which are equally valid in all parts of the West. Generally, where speech difficulties and dyslexias are concerned, parents do well to accept help from the guidance center. Problems are more likely to arise where the help involves family therapy or the treatment of emotional and behavioral disorders. Here everything will depend on the background and personality of the therapist concerned. If parents are uneasy, however, they still face the problem of where to find suitable help in the community.

Choosing from the Potpourri

To the onlooker it must seem confusing. Increasing numbers of professions are getting into the act of helping people by listening to them and making wise and helpful comments. Unhappily there are rivalries not only between the distinct professions but among various groups within each profession. Thus an analytically oriented psychiatrist will feel more akin to an analytically oriented social worker than to a fellow psychiatrist who leans more toward behavioral psychology.

How then can a troubled parent select from the potpourri of professions, qualifications, theoretical orientations and personalities the person most likely to be of help? And as I asked at the beginning of the chapter, should help be sought at all? Let me make a few suggestions.

1. *Your child must want help.* With younger children the rule does not necessarily hold. You can win a younger child over and influence him or her for good. But the older children grow, the more important is the rule that they must want help if they are to get it. By the time children are in their late teens, no experts are going to set matters right unless the help is warmly welcomed and eagerly made use of.

Many parents bring me rebellious teen-agers with the plea, "Please change her, doctor!" But I can't change anyone who doesn't want to be changed. It is quite another matter if the teen-ager says, "I don't know why I act the way I do and I want to change. Please help me." But such a desire is a sine qua non for professional help. And if the root of the trouble lies in fouled up communications in the family as a whole, then the members of the family must likewise recognize that they are involved in the problem and be eager to work at it.

Professionals are not magicians. At best they can assess accurately and give valuable pointers. Don't consult them unless those with problems are prepared to resolve them.

2. *Check with a family physician or a pastor.* If you already know of a competent Christian counselor, consult him. But if not, your family doctor may have an idea whether it is medical help or nonmedical help you need. Your minister as well as your physician will have a more adequate grasp of community resources than you and be able to point to the particular person who can best help. They may also know which of the local professionals or clinics, while not themselves Christian, are sympathetic toward the faith of their clients.

3. *Do not refuse help because it comes from a non-Christian.* I can sympathize with those of my correspondents who will not contemplate help from a non-Christian. I can fully understand that a Christian will have more confidence in a fellow

believer. Yet from my vantage within the profession, having talked with scores of my colleagues about their own faith and the faith of their patients, I know that many of them have genuine respect for a faith they do not share. They would regard it as a gross breach of professional ethics to do or say anything that would undermine Christian (or any other) faith. I wish I could make the same claim for all my colleagues, but I cannot.

There is something else you should think of. We have a proverb: The looker-on sees most of the game. We fool ourselves as Christians into believing that non-Christians are unable to understand our words and actions. While this may be true some of the time, non-Christians see through us a good deal of the time precisely because they look at us with worldly-wise eyes. We close our minds at many points to the conviction of the Holy Spirit to such a degree that he has to use a non-Christian mouthpiece to point out where we are fooling ourselves.

4. *Be more concerned about the person than the qualifications.* This point bears repetition. All the qualifications in the world are not worth as much as experience. If one of my own children needed help I would (if the choice lay between the two) choose a warm, firm, understanding and experienced social worker—even one without a degree—rather than a brilliant psychiatrist recently qualified from the best school in the country. I would also choose a competent and experienced non-Christian over an inexperienced Christian.

Keys to the Strong Room
However valuable professional help may be and however enlightening a book of this sort may prove, neither is a substitute for the warm embrace of a fellow Christian with first-hand experience of your problem and a determination to stand with you. Parents who are drowning in seas of darkness need to be pulled from the water by human hands. In the

words of one of my correspondents, they need "flesh-and-blood arms" around them and "flesh-and-blood brains" to counsel them. Yet where can such an embrace be found outside the ranks of professionals?

In our own distress, Lorrie and I looked vainly for help. We did not lack sympathetic Christian friends, but they did not possess the kind of wisdom we needed. We seemed perpetually to be several steps ahead of them, even though we ourselves were groping in darkness. But in God's mercy some of them supported us in practical ways. We shall never cease to be grateful for their kindness.

Perhaps God desired us to think and pray through the issues carefully ourselves, for without "strong crying and tears" a book of this sort could not have been written. The pathway to peace may have been engraved deeply on our minds in order that "we may be able to comfort those who are in any affliction, with the comfort with which we ourselves are comforted by God" (2 Cor. 1:4). I have known the joy of watching smiles break slowly over parents' tear-stained faces as release has come to them from bondages I have grappled with myself.

You may need such human help. Where can you find it? Of course you have access to God. But Christ has set you among Christian brothers and sisters so that you should comfort them and be comforted by them, teach them and be taught by them, sustain them and be sustained by them. Do not be too proud or too reticent to look for help, for God speaks through his people.

Nor should you yield to discouragement if at first you are disappointed. Look further. Don't limit God. Help may come from an unexpected source, from someone outside your church, from someone even whose views and lifestyle you may question. Elijah was fed and sheltered first by a starving widow and later by ravens.

For some special reason God may call on you as he did on us to grapple with your problems without the comfort of human support. Yours may be the exceptional case in which divine aid makes human help superfluous. But God plans to touch most of us through human fingers and to speak to us through human voices. Help may even come from fellow sufferers who, like you, still grope for answers. Look for other parents in pain and don't be afraid to expose your own pains to them. The relief of finding they are not alone may be of incalculable help.

The people who will help you most may in fact be parents who still struggle. Many years ago when I worked in a bank, our early morning ritual consisted of meeting before the massive doors of the strong room. Five of us each had a different key so that only when all of us were present could we gain access to the strong room. The absence of any one of us seriously hampered the day's work.

Let those of us then who are troubled seek one another out. Alone our progress may be hampered by rigid doors of steel. But the same doors may yield in moments when we bring our different skills and insights to share with one another.

8
In Trouble with the Law

*T*he appearance of a patrol car in front of the house or a telephone call from a police station is often as frightening for you as it is for the son or daughter in trouble. The law can be intimidating if you know nothing about it. Many Christians are especially vulnerable to miscarriages of justice because of their respect for Paul's admonition to be "subject to the governing authorities" (Rom. 13:1).

What should Christian parents do when they find one of their children has been involved in illegal activity? Phone the police? Insist that the child phone the police? What if police ask the parents' permission to talk to your son or daughter alone? Or what if you receive a summons to appear in court? Should you get a lawyer? But if your son or daughter is guilty, is not the Christian attitude one of accepting the just sentence imposed by a court?

Christians, as I have said, tend to respect authority and to show a greater readiness to collaborate with legal authorities than non-Christians. Yet the more you know about the law and its enforcement, the more clearly you see that issues are far from being black and white.

Seeking Justice

The law is people: police officers, judges, lawyers, jailers, probation officers. And people vary. The law's attempt to preserve peace and establish justice is far from perfect. Law reform in many parts of the West is the talk of the day. Even if laws and their past interpretations are just and true, they are administered by sinners. Though many of them are respectable and try to be conscientious, they are sinners nonetheless. Others are outright scoundrels, and yet others are simply inefficient. It follows that laws and their execution fall short of doing what they aim to do. People go to jail (and even get hanged) who shouldn't. Others who deserve to be locked up go free. I could say similar things about any profession or area of civic life, and what I say must not be construed as an attack on the law industry. People everywhere are fallible and sinful.

What attitude then should Christians have before the law? An examination of Romans 13:1-7 seems to make it plain that in general the Christian attitude to law is one of collaboration and of civil obedience. In spite of the fact that some who administer and execute the law may be unjust, Paul points out that first, they are out to catch evildoers rather than honest people, and second, the whole system is sovereignly overruled, indeed, appointed by God.

When Romans 13 is compared with other passages, however, we find that the matter is not so simple. Where human edicts go against God's laws, Christians obey God. "We strictly charged you not to teach in this name [of Jesus]," thundered the high priest, only to receive from Peter and his colleagues the retort, "We must obey God rather than men" (Acts 5:28-29).

Paul at Philippi created quite a fuss when he was wrongfully (that is, without a trial) put in jail. He refused to accept a release unless the city magistrates came down to the jail to release him and Silas in public admission of their wrongful act (Acts 16:35-39). Paul also used his legal rights as a means of getting to Rome (Acts 25:25) and defended himself in court on more than one occasion. It would seem that his teaching in Romans was not inconsistent with using legal means to attain justice or to protest injustice on the part of authority.

A good principle then is: Do not accept every accusation from the authorities but on occasion use legally appointed means to defend yourself and your family. The object in doing so should not be to evade the just penalties of wrongdoing but to avoid misrepresentation of your acts and unjust treatment of them.

The moment I bring up unjust sentences a further question arises. How is a "just penalty" decided in law? Who says what is just and what is unjust? In minor matters in criminal law a magistrate might make the decision simply on the police report and the plea of guilty by the offender. But in general the decision is arrived at by means of an "adversary procedure" in which two experts interpret the law, one representing the plaintiff (in civil law) or the state or crown (in criminal law) and the other representing the defendant.

Let us suppose you are caught absent-mindedly walking out of a store without paying for your purchase. (This is a constant nightmare to me since I am very absent-minded when I go shopping.) Technically you are guilty of shoplifting. If a great deal of shoplifting has been going on at the time, the courts may be getting angry about the practice and sentences may be getting stiffer. How do we decide what would be a just sentence for you?

Your lawyer might feel, and perhaps rightly, that it was an honest mistake and that you should be granted a plea of "not guilty" (provided local laws could so be interpreted in your case). But the prosecuting attorney might have very different thoughts about the matter. So a kind of haggling takes place. You (along with other witnesses) may be examined and cross-examined to establish both what actually took place and what would be a just resolution. "Just sentence," then, is not a concrete reality but a compromise hammered out among several people. Probably with two lawyers pressing their cases, the sentence is generally more just than it would otherwise be. You run the risk of an unjust sentence if you have no knowledge of law and attempt to defend yourself.

Investigating the Police
In general, we should work with authorities since police usually try to cut down crime and to defend honest citizens. But police are often hard pressed to do their duty and sometimes rightly feel they are trying to make bricks without straw. It may happen then that police get overzealous or careless about the rights of juvenile offenders. And it sometimes happens that they are unjust. There are bad cops just as there are bad doctors and bad preachers. Let the following examples act as cautions to blind trust.

Sixteen-year-old Glen one day told his parents that he had broken into a store and stolen several packages of cigarettes. His Christian parents phoned the police who asked to talk alone with Glen. The police were grateful for the opportunity since Glen confessed to five similar offenses occurring during the previous six weeks. None of the offenses would have been detected had Glen not confessed.

The police did not bully Glen in any way. They commended him on his honesty and his collaboration and said they thought that his willingness to own up would help him in court.

Unhappily it didn't help him. His sentence to a juvenile center with a very bad reputation was a long one. And it subsequently turned out that Glen had been led by older boys on the first five occasions. Had this last fact been known, his sentence might have been different. Glen had been trying to protect his friends. He needed counsel (which he never got) about the folly of "taking the rap" due to a false sense of loyalty. And his parents had to pay for six plate glass windows that cost them about $250 each. Had the other boys been apprehended, all would have had to share equally in the cost.

If Glen's parents had known better they would not have given the police permission to question Glen alone. It was good that his guilt became apparent, but it was not good that he received the sentence he did. Nor was it good that his parents had to pay as much as they did.

The center for juvenile detention had an appalling effect on Glen. He went there frightened and repentant but came out a tough little delinquent who is still going strong. A good lawyer might have suggested an alternate and less harmful sentence, not only for Glen's but for society's sake.

Harry's parents became aware that their fifteen-year-old son had been pushing marijuana when they received threatening telephone calls from the gang for whom Harry was a pusher. Evidently Harry had dropped his first and only shipment because he was scared. He left it in a city bus, hopped off and ran, feeling sure that the man sitting behind him was a police officer. Consequently, he had no money to pay his creditors and hence the threatening phone calls. In his desperation he turned to God.

Harry's parents were both doctors. City police were not too involved in drug traffic but the state police, who were, had during the previous six months raided three doctors' homes and one lawyer's home on suspicion that the children there possessed drugs. In searching they removed carpets, tore up floorboards and tore out paneling, doing in all many thousands of dollars' worth of damage for which there was no legal redress. The police found nothing in three of the homes. The phenomenon was a local one and evidently had to do with the local detachment of the state police.

Harry's parents therefore decided not to contact the police but to use as a mediator with the gang, a converted ex-con who "knew the drug scene." Once the gang had received the cost of the dropped shipment and was convinced that Harry was pulling out of drugs, the threats ceased.

I would not care to debate the rights and wrongs of what Harry's parents did except to comment that they might have done better to consult a lawyer. Certainly their mistrust of the state police was understandable. Ask yourself what you would do if your only son had committed a minor delinquency and the result of your collaboration with the police would entail extensive damage to your home, damage you knew would not be justified since no drugs were hidden in your home. The ex-con in question collaborated regularly with state police and from his knowledge of them advised against contacting them.

Examining the Prosecuting Attorney

As caution must be used in dealing with the police, so with prosecuting attorneys. Some have a genuine dedication to exercising justice with a view to discouraging crime. Others need the job satisfaction of winning cases and seem not to care to what lengths they go in doing so.

A young man exposed himself to Sandy, a nine-year-old girl. He stopped his car, opened the door and displayed his genitals. When she walked away, he drove off. Sandy told her mother who called the police who in turn took a statement from Sandy.

Apparently the exhibitionist was already in custody by the time the police came round to the house. He had been practicing his behavior for several weeks to teen-age girls and some older women, many of whom were quite willing to testify in court.

Sandy was a nervous and sensitive little girl who couldn't sleep after the incident. "It wasn't the man, the man that did that thing," she said. "I was scared of the police who asked me all those questions. I didn't want to talk about it." Her mother assured her she wouldn't have to.

But her mother had not counted on the prosecuting attorney who in his zeal wanted every possible witness in court.

152

He displayed no interest in the possible effects of court on Sandy. Only after getting a psychologist's report (a further ordeal for Sandy but not nearly as severe as court might have been) did Sandy's mother avoid a court appearance for Sandy.

The moral is not that prosecuting lawyers, D.A.'s and attorney generals' departments are bad. We need them. They perform a very valuable social function. Rather it is that we are unwise to assume naively that they have everyone's best interests at heart. At times we need to contest their claims.

A seventeen-year-old girl who was rapidly becoming an alcoholic confessed voluntarily to breaking into four liquor stores to steal whiskey for her personal consumption. On each occasion she had hid the liquor and consumed it whenever she could get out at night. Her Christian parents were greatly disturbed about her drinking and at a loss to control it. They were even more disturbed when they found out what she had done.

They lived in a Canadian province where teen-agers are handled in juvenile courts until the age of eighteen. In juvenile courts delinquencies are dealt with confidentially, thus not giving rise to a criminal record. The parents immediately took steps to get psychiatric help for their daughter who also agreed to take a daily dose of Antabuse as long as she remained at home.

Because of "the serious nature of the offense," the lawyer from the attorney general's office appealed to the juvenile court that the offenses be raised to adult court. The girl lacked only nine months to her eighteenth birthday. However, the offenses were her first, she had voluntarily confessed and had sought help for her alcohol problem. Moreover, she had a right to the same protection as other juveniles, many of whom had longer records and had committed more serious crimes. The possible consequences of being raised to adult court were enormous. The girl would then have a criminal record which could affect her chances of employment for life. The critical

question was, Did her offenses truly warrant such consequences? Wisely the parents sought legal counsel. The plea
from the attorney general's department was contested, and
the court agreed with the defense lawyer that it would be more
just and in the best interests of all concerned for the girl to be
tried in juvenile court. The issue at stake was not whether the
offenses should be punished but what the just way of dealing
with them was.

Judging the Judge
Judges vary too. Some are more severe than others. Some believe in treatment while others incline toward retribution.
Some are just and some (a minority in most areas in the West)
are unjust.

Even though they may strive for consistency, judges' moods
will vary. Old hands in the courtroom may shake their heads
after the morning's work is over and say, "His honor's in a bad
mood today," or, "I've never seen him let anyone off that
lightly before." This again should indicate to us that it is not
always easy to determine what constitutes a just sentence.

Many lawyers do their best to find out which judge is presiding in what courtroom on a given day so as to get their
clients on certain dockets. Occasionally a tug of war takes
place between the prosecution and the defense as to when a
trial will take place and who will try the case where.

Christian parents whose children are facing courts will have
no say in such struggles, but they may become aware of them
and grow anxious. Such parents should not concern themselves overmuch with presiding judges but rather should pray
that God so overrule that whoever the judge may be, justice
tempered by mercy shall prevail.

Consulting a Lawyer
When should parents consult a lawyer? And whom should
they choose when they do?

Probably some of the ground we have already covered has begun to answer the first question. You should hire a lawyer whenever you go to court and, many lawyers would add, before any interrogation by police or other officials takes place. As you probably know from watching TV, police caution the people they have detained that they may incriminate themselves by their answers. But in the anxiety and intimidation felt by a minor undergoing a first arrest, such technical details (as the power to remain silent until a lawyer is present) fly away in the breeze.

The cost of hiring a lawyer makes some parents nervous too. In most places in North America lawyers and law students contribute time to some legal aid society. Generally parents will not get the same quality of counsel at such a society as they would by hiring a private lawyer because much of the work is done by less experienced people acting under supervision. In some ways the legal aid society's operation is analogous to that of some emergency rooms in large city hospitals where medical students, interns and junior residents may do a great deal of the work as part of their training. In both cases there is (or should be) supervision by an experienced senior. But help from an inexperienced person under pressure of time and under supervision is not the same as help from an experienced person who has time and energy to devote to the case.

If you as a Christian are able to choose a lawyer, what qualities ought you to look for? It's easy enough to say, "Get a good lawyer!" but what do "good" lawyers look like?

I suppose our answers might differ a little. Most Christians instinctively go for Christian lawyers first, feeling more certain that they will be understood by fellow believers. And certainly this is something to consider. Personally I am less concerned with the lawyer's faith than with his or her personal integrity and professional competence. I would also, if I had the choice, choose a more experienced lawyer over an inexperienced one. My choice then would be among lawyers who put honesty and integrity high on their list and who are more interested in serving justice than in scoring points. Their competence and experience (perhaps in a particular field) would also be important to me. One doesn't consult a tax lawyer about shoplifting or a divorce lawyer about purchasing real estate. Lawyers who have teen-age children of their own may well have a special interest in helping.

I cannot advise you on how to start your search. Most people prefer to be recommended to a lawyer by a friend. Storefront law offices are sprouting in many areas, and they could be a place to start. The lawyers you approach may not be willing to accept your case, either because they are too busy or because your problem is one they prefer other lawyers to handle. Usually they will answer your queries about the names of suitable lawyers.

The Treacherous Three
We may feel anxious before a visit to a professional expert. And if doctors' and dentists' offices awaken inner alarm bells, the noise cannot be compared with the clamor that breaks loose in our skulls when we face our first encounter with the law. We should realize, however, that an experience which threatens to destroy and humiliate us can also make us more mature and poised. Everything depends on how we view matters. A summons to court may be looked on as an unmitigated catastrophe or as a gateway to personal growth and to a more lively trust in God.

The issue will be determined by the way we handle three treacherous emotions: fear, guilt and shame. If these three conquer us we are lost. But if we conquer them our experience will be turned to our profit.

Fear is our first enemy. Our victory will begin when we look him in the eye. We must simply face the fact we are afraid. We need not ask ourselves what we are afraid of. Fear feeds on fantasy, and fantasy is an artist skilled in painting unreal horrors. Time spent in viewing them leads to being waltzed through the night in the arms of terror.

We must turn from fantasy to reality. The question "What do I fear?" must be reworded to, "What is there to fear?" What has changed since the police appeared on my doorstep or since I received a summons to appear in court? "The LORD is my light and my salvation; whom shall I fear? The LORD is the stronghold of my life; of whom shall I be afraid?" (Ps. 27:1). Has my child's brush with the law changed my relationship with God? Must I equate a court summons with divine abandonment? Or are the inviolable walls still around me? Could he who said "I will never leave you, nor forsake you" break his word?

Even the fact that our children might receive severe sentences does not imply that God has abandoned us. His presence will go with us and (if we let him) he will give us peace.

Scripture has a lot to say about fear. "Fear not!" is one of the commonest commands in the Bible. And perhaps the deepest lesson about fear is the one Jesus himself taught. "Do not fear those who kill the body but cannot kill the soul; rather fear him who can destroy both soul and body in hell" (Mt. 10:28). It is true that he was addressing a problem slightly different from the one faced by the parent of a guilty teen-ager. Yet the principle still holds. We fear people (police officers, judges, magistrates) in the degree that we fail to fear God. Whatever the word *fear* may mean (respect, reverence, or terror) Jesus teaches that we have a choice in the direction in which we may turn it and of the objects we choose to attach it to. We may not always be able to quench it, but at least we can choose whether we will fear court officials or Yahweh. Let us then be God-fearing parents who use frightening experiences to teach ourselves what the fear of God means and who learn to be free from "the fear of man."

"What if it's my fault though?" is the question that haunts

us when we grope for inner assurance. Hard on the heels of fear marches guilt. We may associate police and courts with the exposure of wickedness. They awaken fears which began in grade school at the thought of a visit to the principal's office.

I have already discussed the matter of our guilt over our children's wrongdoing. It goes without saying that we are imperfect parents. It is also true, as I have insisted all along, that our children have minds of their own and can make decisions for themselves and that we must not assume all the blame for what they have done. But the sight of a police uniform or the thought of a magistrate's bench may reawaken feelings of guilt we once thought we had put an end to.

Guilt feelings must be dealt with promptly and firmly. Take them before the highest court of all. Any parental failures you are guilty of had wider consequences than those you now face. They led to the death of the Son of God. The sentence for your failure has already been passed and the penalty paid. You should then face earthly courts with your head held high, no longer wrapped up with your failures, but with your attention focused on the fears, the guilts and the shame of your children. The last thing children need when they deal with the law is a guilt-ridden parent. If ever parents need to have boldness before the throne of grace and freedom to be concerned with their children's fears it is when those same children face earthly courts.

Shame is the final and most treacherous enemy of all. Shame seals our lips when we need the prayer support of fellow Christians and makes us turn our backs in bitterness on the children who have dragged our names in the mud. We are ashamed because we think people will despise us for what has happened, and we try to conceal all we can from people we know. We evade discussion. We may even be tempted to bribe our way out of scandal.

Foolishly we may have based our shame on fantasy, the

fantasy of what we imagine people think rather than the knowledge of what they do think. Some are more likely to admire us for our courage in adversity than to look down on us. But the matter goes deeper than fantasies. Our problem with shame is similar to the one we faced with fear. At its root is a wrong attitude to God and to our fellow men and women. We are more anxious about people's opinion than we are about God's. Like the fearful religious leaders of Jesus' day we love "the praise of men more than the praise of God" (Jn. 12:43). So our shame should alert us to the fact that we need to change such an attitude, deliberately concerning ourselves more with what God thinks than with what others do. God is not ashamed of us or of our children, and neither must we be.

Fear, guilt and shame are persistent enemies who may visit us in the night or greet us when we get out of bed in the morning. They must be dismissed firmly and repeatedly. They have only as much power as we are willing to lend them, and if we learn nothing else from our trials than how to conquer all three, we will certainly emerge stronger.

Trouble with the law. I hope it never comes to you. But if it does, take heart. The God of Scripture is revealed as a lover both of justice and of mercy, a defender of the oppressed and a champion of the poor. Whether you win justice for your child or not in the immediate future, his eye is upon you and yours. Ultimately he will redress all wrongs.

As for the nightmare you may feel you are going through, it may prove, as you look to God, to be a valuable learning experience in a dark valley. And the valley will eventually broaden to fertile and sunny pastures where you may experience the bounty of God as never before.

Beyond Pragmatism

9
Relinquishment

*F*or many years we have paid too much attention to *what works* and too little to *what is right*. What is right may or may not work. If we were laboratory animals or computers, the right would be determined by what works and morality would bow to function. But we live in a moral universe, a universe made by a righteous God and inhabited by creatures who have often failed to respond to the way he has "handled them," who have instead chosen the opposite of what he wished. This God calls us to be to our children what he is to us.

Therefore we are not to base our relationship with them on any supposed results of the relationship but on what is right. It follows that if God's greatest desires for his creatures have not always been fulfilled, our desires for our children may not always be fulfilled either. It is better that we aim at being godly parents even though we may fail to produce perfect children, than that we aim at being social scientists employing techniques which, were they successful, would change the parent/child relationship to a technician/object relationship.

We are called to move beyond pragmatism to a walk before

God. We are to choose what is right without demanding that the right shall always gratify our vanity, satisfy our carnal longings or even the yearnings of our least selfish loves. If God has wept over a rebellious humanity, then we at times may have to grieve over rebellious children.

As we look then at ways to correct our parental attitudes, I shall not ask, Do they work? but, Do they reflect God's mind? Are they characterized by faithfulness, justice, long-suffering, chastisement, mercy, love and grace? As the child becomes an adult we must be willing to let him or her reap the consequences of headstrong actions even though our own pain may be greater than the child's. God made Adam who begot Cain. Christ numbered among his intimate trainees a Judas. These next five chapters, then, constitute a re-evaluation of godly parental attitudes.

Nightingales Enslaved

In days gone by market men in Covent Garden, London, used to sell caged nightingales. They captured the birds and blinded them by inserting hot needles into their eyes. Because nightingales sing in the dark, a liquid song bubbled almost endlessly from the caged and blinded birds. Man had enslaved and blinded them to gratify his delight in their music. More than this he had enslaved them in such a manner that they could never again enjoy freedom. No one could set them free.

To relinquish our children is to set them free. The earlier we relinquish them the better. If we unthinkingly view them as objects designed for our pleasure, we may destroy their capacity for freedom just as the Covent Garden men made nightingales "unfreeable." We may also cripple ourselves. Having made our children necessary to our happiness, we can so depend on them that we grow incapable of managing without them.

Yet what is relinquishment? Clearly it must not mean avoiding our parental responsibilities. Our children need food, shelter, clothing, love and training, and it is our business to give them these. Nor does relinquishment mean to fail to teach our children respect and gratitude. Moreover, if we have the responsibility of their upbringing, we must have the authority to do whatever is necessary to fulfill that responsibility.

To understand what relinquishment is we must first understand what God is like and what the essence of his relationship to us is. As he is to us, so must we (so far as possible) be to our children.

God's attitude as a parent (which I discuss again in chapter twelve) combines loving care and instruction with a refusal to force our obedience. He longs to bless us, yet he will not cram blessings down our throats. Our sins and rebellions cause him grief, and in his grief he will do much to draw us back to himself. Yet if we persist in our wrongdoing he will let us find by the pain of bitter experience that it would have been better to obey him.

To relinquish your children does not mean to abandon them, however, but to give them back to God and in so doing to take your own hands off them. It means neither to neglect your responsibilities toward them nor to relinquish the authority you need to fulfill those responsibilities. It means to release those controls that arise from needless fears or from selfish ambitions.

Pride and Privilege

Relinquishment means *to forsake the right to be proud*. Notice, I said "the right to be" proud. It is normal to want children you can be proud of. Sometimes your ambitions for them may become their ambitions too. But you do not have the right to demand that they fulfill your dreams for them.

"Haven't I fed and clothed them?" some parents say. "Didn't I bring them into the world? Who paid for their education? Who worked their fingers to the bone so that they could get extra training in sports, in music, in horseback riding? And look what they've done to me...."

Such parents may indeed have given their children more than they needed, more than even the best of parenting calls for. But why did they do so? Were they perhaps paying a high price to have their own dreams vicariously gratified? Unconsciously they may have wanted to realize in their children's lives something they failed to realize in their own. Yet the life they were dreaming about was not their own but their children's—or better, God's. If anyone had a claim to rights in their lives, he had. Yet even God would not force his righteous claims on them.

Yet it is painful to sit silently while other parents tell of their children's triumphs. It is not easy to have achieved success ourselves in a certain area and to see other people's children succeed in the same area while our own children fail. It is easier to reproach them, to sit over them as they do their school assignments, never letting a word or a number escape our jealous eyes in our endeavor to assure their academic success. It is easier to holler at them during hockey practice or swimming practice, or to push them into the religious limelight. We may call our frantic coaching and tutoring "help." But what motivates the help? Is it our need to triumph through our progeny?

You may argue that without an education your children will suffer want or that games are good for the development of their self-respect and their character. But that is beside the point. What motivates the anxiety with which some parents encourage such development?

How reassuring it is to be congratulated about what your children do or how they dress or what salary they get or into what family they marry. "He's a real credit to you." "I wish my daughter were like Jane." "Your son Tom has extremely good manners." "Cynthia has done tremendously well to pull off a job like that! She's certainly turned out to be a girl you can be proud of! Who knows how far she'll go!" "Aren't you proud to have two missionary sons and a daughter who's a pastor's wife?"

Who would not want such accolades? Yet some parents get no accolades. Instead they grieve as their hopes burst one by one. To them it seems that every effort they put into raising the children was wasted. They swallow their shame as they mingle with the parents of successful children.

Give up your right to be proud. Things could turn out better than you hoped but it is not for that reason I urge it. Your children were not given to you in order for you to boast. Let your boast be in God's goodness to them and to you, in all he has taught you through them and in the privilege he gave you of watching over them. What greater privilege could there be than to be entrusted with care for a new life from God?

Prison Cottages

Relinquishment also means *to give up the right to uninterrupted enjoyment of your children.* Children bring joy as well as pain. Even to look at them may cause a surge of unexpected happiness. To watch them grow, to observe new things they learn and new skills they acquire, to listen to their first secrets and confidences, to share in and help them solve their first problems, to observe them as they enjoy themselves at a family gathering, to find they have emerged from a so-called phase that you thought would never end, to share their triumphs and joys, to see them become men and women—these things and many others can be immense sources of enjoyment.

But we can poison enjoyment unless we are prepared to relinquish our right to it. I know a wealthy Christian who owns property by a lake. The summer cottages of his sons and daughters surround his own. He paid for and gave them to his children so he could have them nearby. "He buys our affection," one son-in-law, who had planned to take his wife far away, complained to me bitterly.

"You don't have to accept his generosity," I pointed out. "But daddy always acts hurt when we don't do what he wants," his wife replied. "He makes us feel so guilty. He sometimes cries and we feel mean and ungrateful."

I do not excuse the children, for they had sold their independence for summer cottages by a lake. But I also see that by insisting on his right to enjoy his children ("he wants all of us round him all the time"), he had clipped their wings. His attitude did not begin only when the children were old enough to marry. Years before he had assumed that it was his right to enjoy his children indefinitely. Slowly he began to demand that they remain as his toys and pets.

I enjoy the robins on my back lawn. I get hugely excited as I watch a mother raccoon and her young sneak by my house on their way to the river. I love to stand at the foot of the grounds to see the badgers and muskrats swimming silently on the river at night or to watch rabbits and squirrels about their business all around us.

I would be sad if they went away. But I have no right to capture them just to keep on enjoying them. Indeed in captivity they would change. Paradoxically, it is only as I relinquish my right to enjoy them that I am free to enjoy them most.

I know a father who sends his sons' letters back unopened if they do not arrive by the first mail on Monday morning. I know other parents who upbraid their children bitterly if letters do not arrive as frequently as they would wish.

Should parents not teach their children filial duty? Of course they should. Should children not be taught to consider, and even eventually to care for their aging parents? Certainly. But this is not what I am talking about. To teach what is right is one thing. To insist that I get my parental "rights" is quite another. We shall be of all men and women most miserable if we demand that our children make us happy or if we depend on them for our delights. What is my motive in writing "hurt" letters or making aggrieved telephone calls? Is it really to help the children? Or is it to vent my spleen? To hurt? To make the children feel sorry for me in my loneliness?

If you are a parent of younger children, you may feel my writing does not at this point apply to you. But you are wrong. The attitudes that seem so ugly in older parents began when they were young parents of small children. And they began with a possessive mindset, the mindset that regards my children as my pets. I may claim that it will be good for the children to learn unselfishly to contribute to my happiness, but let me be absolutely honest with myself. Is my first concern really with their moral development or is it with my own needs?

Joy in my children may be my privilege, but it is never my right. If I have claimed it as a right, I must relinquish it. In doing so I shall avoid needless disappointment and tension. But it is not because it makes me feel better (not because it works) that I insist, but that I might please the Father by a more godly attitude to my children. I may grieve when they fail to come home for Christmas, when they join another church, when they marry inappropriately or when they seem to forget me. God shares my sorrow. But if I have renounced the right to enjoy my children, my sorrow will have no taint of bitterness.

Relinquishment, of course, also means *to give up my right to possess my children.* I do not and must not *own* them. I knew a widow who clung to her daughter. Both were Christians. "It is your duty to stay with me," the mother would say. "You must obey me because I am your mother." She decided on the tasks her daughter was to carry out, on the clothes she must wear, on the times she must leave or return to the house, on whom she could speak to or associate with until her daughter, at the age of thirty rebelled and left her mother—filled with guilt at the "sin" she committed in doing so.

So pathological an example of parental abuse would seem

to offer little instruction were it not for the fact that the abuse sprang from a wrong attitude toward her daughter which she had entertained from the child's infancy. It became clear when I talked with her that she viewed her daughter as her possession and that she had always done so. But her daughter was only someone entrusted to her care. She was not her slave. She did not own her. I may keep my daughter at home because she is not yet ready to face the world alone, because she has not yet acquired skills to care for herself properly and is not emotionally ready to be denied the family's close support. But she is developing rapidly and as soon as she is able and wants to, I must let her go. She is not my possession. She was loaned to me for training.

Canceling All Debts

Relinquishment means *to be willing to forego any repayment for what you have done for your children.* To care for the aged and infirm is beautiful. It is a trait which distinguishes humans from the animals. Sadly, in modern urban society the care of the aged is becoming increasingly the responsibility of the state and the occupation of paid professionals. Ideally it is the happy prerogative of the immediate family, in whose home grandparents and great-grandparents can spend what powers they have left sharing in household joys and responsibilities. Modern conditions may make the ideal impossible, as may infirmity or the temperament of the aging parent.

May we then look to our children to care for us in our old age? Is our care of them an investment to be cashed in the future? Do we look to them for repayment of our care, our prayers, our heartaches, our labors, our fortunes? Ought not our children to be taught their duty to support us when we cannot care for ourselves?

Parents differ widely in their feelings about the subject, regardless of their attitudes to their own old age, some vowing "I'll never be a burden to them," others wanting some return for all they have done. But among many parents lingers the feeling that their children owe them something, owe them in fact a great deal.

"But I want my children to learn to care for and love old people," some may say. It is a worthwhile goal. The best way children can learn to care for the aged is to watch you in your own attitude toward your parents or the parents of your spouse. If your care for your own parents is a joy and a delight, then it will be natural for your children to respond to you in the same way. If, on the other hand, your aged relatives are a trial or a responsibility you resent, you can be sure that they will store in their minds the relationship you model for them.

Your children may seem to take you for granted, but it is better so than that they mistrust or fear you. If they have children, their hearts will move out in love to their children more than to you. For a long time yet they are going to think more of what they can expect from you than of what you can expect from them. Let them pass on to their children whatever you have given to them, just as you passed on to your children what your parents gave to you. Don't cling to your right to gratitude, for then if gratitude comes you will be overjoyed. Demand it and you may grow bitter. Renounce your right to birthday cards and presents, to Christmas gifts, to anniversary surprises. Firmly give up to God your claim on any of these things.

Your children owe you a great deal. By all means teach them to express gratitude. Nevertheless, to look for gratitude from them because you yearn to savor it is to poison your relationship. Relinquish your right to their gratitude.

Relinquishment means *to give up your right to uninterrupted tranquility.* It is worthwhile to teach your children to respect order, but to have children will almost certainly mean that you will have problems. The problems may be large or small. They will arise when you least expect them. They will pay no heed to your plans, your convenience, your schedule, your health, your headaches, your finances. Children do not consider your need for a relaxing tub bath when they break a leg, nor for a deadline you are rushing to meet when they vomit on your study carpet. Their school problems or their problems with the police will not wait until an important visitor leaves the house.

There are times when you can and should insist that your needs and even your wishes take priority over your children's demands. But if your peace depends on so controlling events that nothing gets out of hand but that everything remains in its place, then either you or your children are going to be in trouble. Probably your tension will rise till you explode.

Give up your right to tranquility. By all means tell the children to turn down their record players or to make less noise. By all means forbid them to swing on the chandeliers. But forfeit all right to immunity from the unexpected, the unlooked for, the unplanned, the disruptive, the bombshell that changes the course of your whole life. Children are not a stream trickling gently through the ordered garden of your life. Give up your right to domestic tranquility. Be grateful for every moment of it as a gracious God gives you to enjoy. Once again it may sometimes be your privilege, but it will never be your right.

Relinquishment will mean *to give up your right to respectability.* I use the term respectability loosely, of course. When I hear someone remark, "Those people are not very respectable," I usually interpret the remark to mean, "I, the snob, am entitled to adopt a condescending attitude to those people because the finger of scandal has touched them. There is a juicy bit of gossip I could tell you about them." To put it another way then: give up your right to immunity from gossip.

May gossip pass you by. But do not cling to your right to escape it. You can (more or less) control your own actions. You can keep your nose clean, stay out of trouble and avoid all appearance of evil. It is not so easy to control your children's actions to the same degree. How can you hold up your head when your daughter's pregnancy becomes obvious? Who knows? What will they think? If you ask such questions, your perspective has become distorted and your relationship with your daughter will be affected.

What is gossip? What is reputation? How much do they really matter? They will not matter a scrap on Judgment Day. Will you shake hands with Mary Magdalene when you meet her? Or will you try not to catch her eye? Would you sit next to the woman taken in adultery if she turned up in your church?

There is a streak of snobbery in most of us. It is comforting to meet with general approval in our social circles. And our children can ruin our chances—or should I say can burst our silly aspirations and embarrass us. That is why it is important for us to give up our right to respectability.

Give up your right to be immune from gossip! Tell God that though you don't want scandal there are things more important in life than "the praise of men."

Relinquishment also means *to allow your children to face pain, tragedy and even death,* and to allow them to accept the consequences of their own actions. You cannot protect children forever. Indeed there is a sense in which you should let them face the consequences of their actions from the first, allowing them to discover more and more of what life is like.

Wealthy parents of alcoholics are known for their mistakes in this regard. They pay their children's debts, bail them out when they await trial, hire expensive lawyers for them, go out on a limb arranging employment for them. Some never seem to learn.

They never let go. The "child" may be in his mid-thirties and have been married and divorced. Yet parents still cover misdemeanors, court expenses and bouncing checks. They should let go. They cannot help their children. Indeed, by protecting them they are preventing their children from

Parents in Pain

learning very valuable lessons—the hard way. To relinquish your children is to let them face life for themselves.

It may be hard to know when a child should accept full adult responsibility. But the process must begin with a willingness on your part to let your children discover at an early stage that fire burns.

Relinquishment means to trust God about your children rather than your own ability to manage their lives. It means recognizing that wise counsel to older children is just that— wise counsel. It cannot be forced on them. It may, and often will, be refused by them.

In a Latin American Taxi

But there is more to relinquishment than all I have outlined so far. At its heart, relinquishment is not relinquishment of your children but of delusions about your own power, the delusion that you have power to determine their destinies.

Two-year-old Stephen accepts the fantasy that while sitting in the car seat with a steering wheel, he is driving the car. For mother and child the delusion is an innocent piece of fun. Stephen can make engine noises and drive in fancy to mummy's destination. But some of us in cars have a less pleasant experience.

Sitting in the front seat of a taxi in some Latin American capitals, I often notice my foot pressing fiercely on the floorboard. As we rock and scream between what seem to be hostile and aggressive vehicles hemming us in or hurtling by us like passing planets, my hands grope for a steering wheel that isn't there or push against the dashboard as if to ward off the back of the truck toward which we are hurtling. I find that the muscles of my stomach are struggling to drive too. Clearly some part of me suffers from the delusion that my movements can ward off danger. My body is trying to control what happens even though my mind is telling it to relax. I must find it in me somewhere to learn how to relinquish the control of the car to my insane chauffeur.

The picture vividly portrays our dilemma as parents. We make the same kinds of futile movements toward our children that I make in Latin American taxicabs.

I once had a patient and her husband staying with us in our home. They came from a great distance, and there was no room for them in the local hospital. Nancy, who had a simple, straightforward condition made an excellent patient with a slow but steady recovery. But Jim....

"Don't you think you should decrease her medication a bit? She told me she gets this funny itch behind her left ear. You know, Nancy isn't like the rest of your patients. I don't think you realize how sensitive she is to medication. She nearly went into a coma last time she had pneumonia. The doctors just couldn't grasp that...."

Or, "I think you ought to get Nancy to play the piano more.... She shouldn't read so much."

Or, "Doctor, I think Nancy has been in the sun too much. The sun usually makes her dizzy and gives her headaches. Could you suggest to her—mind you, you're the doctor and I'm only suggesting—could you suggest to her that she try to sit in the shade more? And could you suggest she take it easy walking?"

Endlessly he organized her day. Some of his messing was harmful, mostly it was irrelevant. The tragedy was that he wore himself out with anxiety and tension because he held the delusion that he was controlling her progress. Needless to say I spent more time calming Jim than curing Nancy.

As parents we do exactly what Jim was doing. With an exaggerated notion of our power to make our children different, to accelerate their development, to change their habits, likes and dislikes, we waste endless nervous energy.

Or we nag. Or we hint endlessly and elaborately. Or we leave significant books lying around accidently, books full of advice our children need. Or we plan to have key people in the house at critical junctures. We scheme. We plot. We wax eloquent and enthusiastic trying to light sparks in our children while we ourselves care not a fig for the things we gush over.

Relinquishment consists of a freeing from a whole series of rights and delusions which are not truly rights at all but costly territorial claims ministering to my discontent and delusions of power over a vehicle driven by another.

If relinquishment were merely a giving up it would be relief enough. But it is giving up *to God.*

I sometimes wonder at the trust of Hannah as she left her tiny Samuel in the charge of old Eli at Shiloh (see 1 Sam. 1:1—2:11). She had relinquished much—her right to possess, to enjoy, to be proud before her rival Peninnah, to control Samuel's development, to be repaid for all her tears. She did not know her son would change the destiny of Israel, towering above the nation's history as the founder of two dynasties of kings, setting the moral tone of the nation for generations to come. The fashioning of such a man was the work of God himself.

I do not know what destiny whether small or great God plans for the children who most concern you. I do know that you will have more peace if you can grasp how crucial relinquishment is, how utterly safe it is to place your children in God's sure hands.

10

From Utopia to Galilee

We live in a society of rising expectations. What once were dreams and luxuries are now needs. The mounting clamor of such expectations threatens to exceed society's capacity to satisfy them.

In a recent article Richard Farson drew attenton to the social repercussions of psychological techniques. One example he used had to do with the effects of teaching better communication between spouses.[1] It used to be enough to get along reasonably well with one's spouse and to have one's material needs met with perhaps a few comforts thrown in. During recent decades we have learned that good communication between spouses is essential to marriage. Books have multiplied popularizing communication techniques and awakening us to the desirability of communicating effectively with our wife or husband. Marital difficulties have been resolved and separations averted as under skillful tutelage spouses have learned to communicate effectively.

Now comes the twist. As Farson points out, the divorce rate has continued to rise during this same period of time. Whereas in years gone by the causes cited for divorce included infidelity, cruelty and incompatibility, during the last fifteen years there has been a dramatic rise in divorces allegedly caused by "poor communication." Communication is in. If their marriage lacks it, then they quit. It seems that by popularizing marital communication, psychologists have raised our expectations of marriage producing what doctors call an *iatrogenic effect* (a new illness caused by medication). The knowledge which may cure ailing marriages has at the same time awakened new dissatisfactions leading to more frequent divorces.

The Parenting Gap

Here then is a paradox. Useful and beneficial discoveries may work evil as well as good. We do well to be concerned with the oppressed and to sacrifice ourselves for them. But in our fervor we must not stir up hunger in a famine or thirst in a drought. We must be wise and realistic as we seek to help our fellow men and women lest in our blind enthusiasm we awaken passions we are unable to assuage.

We hear, for example, talk of "child rights" or "a bill of rights for children." These things are good. Yet the world being what it is and parents being what they are, we must beware of naïve optimism, of assuming that because we can delineate a problem we have solved it. What parents *should* give their children and what parents *are capable of* giving their children are not the same thing. With all the good will and enlightenment in the world, many parents will still not be able to provide what we might see as desirable for child development. Merely to tell them what they should do might only drive them to despair. And despairing or desperate parents are the worst parents of all.

Even in the basic matter of food and shelter, the West has yet to achieve satisfactory standards of child care. To be sure, we are far ahead of the rest of the world. Yet our slums swarm with undernourished, inadequately clothed children

—children whose condition may not always be blamed on their parents. I mention the fact only because in matters of food and shelter the state can (in theory at least) provide necessities the parents cannot. But the state cannot tuck children into bed at night and pray with them. The state is largely powerless to provide the emotional warmth, the consistent discipline, the sense of being wanted and accepted that should be the prerogatives of every child. These things must be provided by parents.

And we parents are imperfect. We are imperfect not only in failing to do those things we can (which is blameworthy) but in lacking some parental capacities entirely. We can only give what we have. We cannot give what we do not have. So our children are bound to experience deprivation because they are born to imperfect parents in a fallen world.

"But surely we must not excuse parents who fail their children! What we must do is urge all parents to meet the highest standards possible!" Of course, but at this point I run into a problem. I find that it is the conscientious parents, the parents who read every book and who try their hardest who are most crippled by their sense of failure.

During recent weeks I have run across two such parents (from two different families), one a man and the other a woman, who were both so distraught by their failures to meet the standards the child-rearing books demanded that they had become largely ineffective as parents. Both were university graduates. One had extra training in child care and development and was a consultant to elementary schools. Both wept as they described their failures with their own children. Both were Christians.

The woman told me she had bought every book she could lay her hands on, both Christian and secular, about how to be a good parent. She had studied them diligently with her husband. They had prayed about resolutions they made as a result of reading the books. But she wept in my office over her apparent inadequacies.

She was, of course, absurdly overanxious about the subject. Nor must we conclude that child-rearing books are to be avoided, any more than we should eschew effective communication in marriage. The lesson to be drawn is that we must not only focus our attention on what children need but on what parents can provide. Usually there is a gap between the two. We need to study what capacities we have in relation to what our children need.

Growing children, for instance, greatly enjoy parents who can play with them—on the lawn or on the rug when they are tiny, or in later years over table games on winter nights or beside a river at dawn with a fishing rod. Some parents are outgoing, gregarious and have a natural affinity for children. To such parents, playing with their children is gratifying and relaxing, an activity to look forward to. Other parents have no idea how to play with children, even their own children. And between the two extremes is a wide range of parental aptitudes for child play. Some fathers are keen on sports and delight in throwing balls in the open air. Other fathers are uncoordinated, shortsighted and unskilled at athletics. Some parents can swim. Others are terrified of water. Some parents can dismember bicycles and repair tires. Others are hopelessly inept. Some fathers work nine to five. Other fathers work shifts.

To do them justice, most writers on child rearing recognize the difficulty. Nevertheless it is impossible to read their books without becoming aware of a ghostly stereotype of the ideal parent, a stereotype few of us can match. Our skills, affinities and timetables vary. What is a delight to one parent is a nightmare to another and impossible to a third. It is not merely a matter of laziness and of failed responsibility, though these too play their part.

Our circumstances also vary. Some parents are overbusy

because they are too keen on money or because they delight in the glamour of being asked to feature in political activities, religious meetings or social festivities. Other parents are exhausted trying to make ends meet. A flood of articles addressed to the former asking them whether money and fame are more important than children may never be read by the very parents who should read them. But you can be sure they *will* be read by those in the latter group who are too weary to do more than keep their children fed, clothed and shepherded between school, table, bathroom and bed. Yet the pious articles tell them that if they are too busy to play with their children, then they are too busy. And what shall we say to the widowed, the divorced and the single parents?

What do children need? And how well can parents meet their needs? Children need acceptance. They need praise and appreciation. They need to learn they can trust their parents not to deceive them or to break promises. They need consistency and fairness. They need to feel that their fears, their desires, their feelings, their inexplicable impulses, their frustrations and their inabilities are understood by their parents. They need to know exactly where the limits are, what is permitted and what is prohibited. They need to know that home is a safe place, a place of refuge, a place where they have no need to be afraid. They need warm approval when they do well and firm correction when they do wrong. They need to learn a sense of proportion. They need to know that their parents are stronger than they are, able to weather the storms and dangers of the outer world and also able to stand up to their (children's) rages and unreasonable demands. They need to feel their parents like them and can take time to listen. They need perceptive responses to their growing need for independence.

We could continue to add to and to amplify the list, but you can see at once that if all these needs are to be met there must be corresponding parental capacities.

Take the need for acceptance for example. Margaret takes to her first baby like an addict to heroin. She glows whenever she looks at her. She doesn't hold the baby, she oozes round her like warm ectoplasm so that the baby floats between her soft ecstatic arms and her equally ecstatic bosom. Mother and baby purr in harmony. They are not two separate beings but a coordinated whole.

Betty, on the other hand, is stiff, tight and uncertain of herself. She seems to have three elbows and to move in spasmodic jerks. Through no fault of her own, Betty will not provide for her baby the same reassuring tactile experiences as Margaret. Betty may try to imitate Margaret like someone trying to copy Peggy Fleming. Margaret's baby will probably feel accepted. Betty's baby just might not. Betty's uncertain grip and hard angles will not reassure the child.

Betty may be distressed about the differences, may feel like a failure, like an inadequate mother. Yet logically no one can blame her. We would probably all assure her that she should not blame herself. But we would have the uneasy feeling that her child has been given a pretty raw deal. While Betty can be encouraged and helped to cultivate a more pneumatic technique for handling him, we realize that he will never have it as good as Margaret's baby.

In a mistaken desire to help Betty's child, we might try to turn lead into gold, to write books teaching Betty how to ooze correctly to fulfill her baby's needs. We might even succeed. The only problem would be that by the time ten thousand mothers like Betty had learned (after exerting much effort and nervous energy) how to ooze (and some mothers never do), their babies would be beyond the stage that called for oozing, and at a stage that called for bouncing and making silly noises, a technique with which they might feel as awkward as they originally did with oozing. Thus mothers like Betty (if we can think of them as a category) would perpetually be slow learners catching up, and their babies forever a disadvantaged child group.

Parenting Takes Practice

This dilemma is a capsule sketch of the dilemma of many parents and their children at many stages of development. I noted earlier that children need a sense of security. But if their parents are themselves insecure, the children's needs will not be met adequately. I noted too that children need consistency. But consistency is not learned overnight. Either you have it or you have to work at it. And while you're still working at it, your children will not derive much benefit from it. Again, I said children need to know where the limits are. But many very good parents only learn themselves where the limits should be by the time they're raising their third child. This makes it rough on child #1 and child #2. In fact child #1 may wind up hating child #3 plus both parents because as child #1 sees it, child #3 can get away with murder. I may be caricaturizing a little, but the facts of real family life are tragicomedy.

Let me go on. Children, I said, need approval when they do well. I could go further. Children need warm approval, lots of it, even when they're doing only passably well. Now even *cold* approval is not always easy to churn out. First, you set out to praise your teen-ager. You are sitting, let us say at the supper table, watching him carefully for the first sign of praiseworthiness. But the more you concentrate the more difficulty you have. He is lounging—rear end on the edge of his chair, shoulders against the back, roughly at the level of the tabletop. You are controlling your rising irritation when he scoops several peas over his front which promptly fall to the floor.

As I sit here in the tranquility of my study writing about your situation, I find it easy to give you advice. You have several options. One would be to control your irritation and to say in a friendly but firm voice, "Sit up properly. Then you'll be able to control your peas better." Then, as he sits up *(if* he sits up), you can move right in with warm praise, "That's the way! That's much better!" or whatever expressions would convey approval and support. You are not, however, sitting with me in my study but at the table. Your irritation grows as you watch the peas spill. Before you can stop yourself you say the wrong thing.

The first option I described is my own favorite. There are others, all with advantages and disadvantages. But let me be honest. It took me quite some time before my favorite option had become routine, though I still get thrown from time to time. But years ago I remember sitting at the table feeling dreadful that *I could not see anything to praise* in my children's table manners. I felt the pain of unrelenting guilt, knowing that something must be wrong with me. Yet try as I might I could do nothing better than spout criticism, strangling my voice into strained gentleness.

Little by little I got the hang of it, and the more I got the hang of it the less irritation I felt. I learned to give positive suggestions and instructions rather than negative criticisms. Gradually praise became not only possible but reflex. I began by praising (whether I felt like praising or not) on the assumption that if praise is merited it should be given. Over the years it got easier though there had to be relearning (on my part) with every new set of behaviors my children acquired. And I am still not immune from a burst of irritation.

Notice. I said *over the years*. I was learning one aspect of parenting. I could figure out the strategy I wanted to follow without much difficulty, but learning to do it took practice. It was like learning to play an instrument. What began as horrendous frustration wound up as joy. But my children were the guinea pigs on whom I did my learning.

For most parents, parenting is an acquired skill, learned (if it is ever learned) through many humiliating mistakes and failures at the expense of its intended beneficiaries. There are no courses in parenting. The theory of parenting is infinitely less important than its practice. Books can tell you what to do, but doing it is another matter. It takes the lifetime of at least one child to learn to cope with the full range of that child's reactions. And the learning you do on one child is by no means guaranteed to be suitable for the next.

Some parents take to the business well. Others are fortunate enough to have tractable children. Yet some of the least gifted parents are by a grim irony allotted children who would be monsters even under the most skillful handling in the world. This is the way life is.

Attitudes and Assets; Lies and Liabilities

If we ought to pay more heed to what is right than to what works and if between child needs and parent capacities there is a gap, what is the godly attitude to adopt? Let me suggest a few principles.

1. *Concentrate on your assets.* Take stock. Make a list of your strengths and weaknesses, but let your focus first be on your strengths. Check the list with your mate or any friend in whom you have confidence. They may see some strengths and abilities you may be unaware of.

As a parent I felt handicapped in the area of sports because, being English, I had not learned Canadian sports and games. By concentrating on what I could do rather than on what I couldn't and by searching for areas with which my skills and my children's capacities for enjoyment coincided, we had many happy hours together. Curiously one of our chief delights was reading together, a practice we continued until my children were well into their teens. They discovered that being read to from a favorite book was much more gratifying than watching TV. I mention the matter not in order to suggest you read to your children, but to emphasize that you should concentrate on what you have more than struggle with what you lack.

Don't be too influenced by magazine stereotypes of an ideal parent. Take your list and thank God for what you have. Some of your strong points may seem to have no potential for helping your children. No matter. Thank God for all he has given you. Praise him as the true source of your assets, all of which come from him.

Tell him you don't want to be like the servant who buried his talent in the soil but that you would like to make full use of your talents. Ask him to show you how. Do so not once but repeatedly for it may take time for you to see how your gifts may benefit your family and yourself.

Remember (as Tim LaHaye has so often pointed out) that what seems like a liability from one standpoint may be an asset from another. Fussiness about details may turn you into a nag if you misuse it but into a careful planner if you use it properly. Ask God to show you the strength behind your weakness and to reveal where and how it may be put to service.

2. *Bring your liabilities to God.* Mourn them without mortification. Mourn them not because they humiliate you or even because they hurt your children but because they are offensive to God. Read Psalm 51 aloud before God. Tell him you have no power whatever to rectify your weaknesses but that you will ever turn in repentance the moment they give rise to sin.

3. *Never pretend to your children that you are better than you are.* Let them know you are a fellow struggler, one who may have known glorious victories but equally ignominious defeats. Don't pretend to be victorious if you are not.

"How can I let Christ down before my children?" you may ask me. If you have let Christ down then you have let him down. But don't multiply your sin by lying to your children about having dishonored him. Christ's glory is not shielded by lies.

I do not say you are to bare your soul to your children, or to reveal to them the horrors of every pit into which you have descended. But where your conduct in the home has been blameworthy, be open about it. And as I urged above, be open about God's grace to you as well. They must not see in you a paragon of virtue but a redeemed sinner, one who goes on learning and who refuses to be discouraged by falls. Give them someone to follow not someone to worship.

4. *Don't brood over your failures.* Yes, your sins and weaknesses have harmed your children, just as your parents' weaknesses harmed you (and just as your children's weaknesses will damage their children, from generation to generation). We do not yet live in the New Earth. The curse, though no longer triumphant, still has power to sting.

But brooding over the damage you have inflicted on your children will help nobody—least of all your children. It is good to recognize your faults. It is better to confess them, yet without morbidity or self-pity but with straightforward honesty to God and to your children.

But then leave it at that. Don't dwell on your sins. Don't cripple yourself with futile remorse. Children are surprisingly resilient. The damage may be less than you think. In any case, God cares for them and for their future far more than you do and is abundantly able to work in their lives. Your children can do without your brooding which reflects nothing except bruised self-esteem.

Brooding also dishonors God. It is not mourning before him but shutting him out of your pain, even blaming him at times. It is an offense that rises like a foul smell toward heaven.

The curse still operates in family relationships. But the redemptive power of Jesus Christ operates where your failures have damaged and go on damaging your children. I do not altogether know how this is so. But I know that no insights are so profound and no liberations so triumphant as those where grace touches the scars and brokenness that come to us by sinful inheritance. And in every weakness your

187

children were born with and in every psychic wound your own sin has inflicted on them lie seeds of miraculous grace. Water those seeds with your prayers and you may one day worship as you see godly strengths and glories spring forth from the very bruises inflicted by sin.

The Loaves-and-Fishes Principle

Throughout this chapter I have been coming to grips with the gap between what your children need and what you have to give them. I maintain there is a gap and nothing will persuade me otherwise. If it were not so, the world would be a Utopia. But there is no child-rearing Utopia. It is to the shores of Galilee we must turn for a lesson in obedience.

I have tried neither to excuse you nor to counsel you to be careless or indifferent. When Jesus stared at a hungry crowd of five thousand people and asked his disciples to feed them, they brought before him in their perplexity five loaves of barley and two small fish, rightly commenting, "But what are they among so many?" The crowd was vast and it clamored for food. Jesus demanded the need be met. It is the same with your children. Their need is great. Your capacity to meet it inadequate.

You must not lament all you lack but must bring what you have to Jesus. It is his job to multiply the bread and the fish. Yours, while recognizing that your offering falls short of what is needed, is to give it to him anyway. Bring what you have and give it to your children. You may seem to be getting nowhere, but the responsibility is now Christ's. You may be surprised how far he will make your little offering go to satisfy your hungry children.

And if there are still needs and lacks, what does it matter? You have done what you could and fulfilled your task. The rest of the responsibility remains with him. But who knows? Perhaps when you are old and are one day counting up your assets, you may be awed to come across twelve baskets of bread and fish among your family treasures.

11
Toward Human Dignity

*I*n the days before we were enlightened about child rearing, when in our ignorance we reared as we had been reared, punishment and discipline were all of a piece. We disciplined when we punished and we punished when we disciplined. Did it matter what name we gave the pain we inflicted on our erring children? Did it matter if a little retribution was mixed in with our correction?

But science looked with disfavor on punishment and exalted discipline. A marriage of centuries was dissolved and punishment was turned into the street. Yet there are signs that the old couple hanker to get together again and that alone each may do more harm than good.

Many books have been written about child discipline both by Christians and non-Christians, but none that I know deals adequately with the issue of punishment. Discipline is generally seen as enlightened and good, punishment as old-fashioned and bad. Parents who think in terms of punishment may be labeled *punitive,* a term synonymous with *hostile, vindictive, vengeful* and *cruel.* Perhaps it is time we re-examined the place of punishment and exercised greater caution before jettisoning such ideas as blame and guilt. None of us wants to defend punitiveness (at least in the sense in which the word is commonly used). But punishment can be administered by patient and merciful people. It is not necessarily the invention of "punitive" people nor are those who give it necessarily being cruel.

Both Discipline and Punishment
The aim of discipline is to train the person being disciplined. Discipline is a means by which that person's behavior may be shaped to please the rest of us and hopefully in a way that will be better for the person receiving the discipline. If a child has the habit of stealing, for example, discipline will aim to make him or her more honest.

Punishment on the other hand aims to rectify an injustice. The person being punished is seen as guilty of a wrong. He or she owes a moral debt to the rest of us. The punishment is viewed as a means of putting the wrong right, repaying the debt and removing the guilt. "You deserved that," a parent might tell a child who is being punished. "I have paid my debt to society," says the criminal who emerges from jail.

Thus whereas discipline aims to help the person disciplined, punishment aims to benefit society, both by meeting its demand that evil not pass unrecognized and by serving as a warning to all would-be wrongdoers. If punishment does anything for the wrongdoer, it will give him or her the sense that "now my wrong is paid for and I can forget about it."

We can see at once why the concept of punishment is out of tune with modern thought. "The idea of punishment is alien to the New Testament," a visiting theologian recently stated to a group of Winnipeg psychiatrists. Whereas at first glance discipline strikes us as a form of mercy by which the disciplined person is helped to a better life, punishment would seem not to have the good of the wrongdoer in mind.

It may not even be clear how society is helped by punishing sinners. While it makes sense to make robbers repay what they have stolen, the only sense in locking them up might be that the rest of us are possibly induced not to steal or that we are kept safe from their misdeeds. Once you say, "It will teach the thief not to steal," you view the imprisonment as treatment (discipline) rather than punishment, and focus on hoped for results rather than justice.

Up to now we have been thinking of discipline as a means of training normal children to live in a normal world. While it is far from easy to define *normal* scientifically, we have as individuals perhaps arrogantly assumed that we can recognize it when we see it. Now whereas normal people are trained to live normal lives by means of discipline, abnormal people are helped to do so by means of *treatment* (which is just another name for what up to now we have been calling discipline). Abnormal behavior is viewed not as bad but as sick. Delinquency and crime thus call for treatment rather than punishment. We would not blame a woman for having cancer but would urge kindness and medical help for her. Therefore (or so the argument runs) we feel it to be more humane not to punish criminals but to see that their condition is given appropriate therapy. In the same way delinquent children are now viewed as having problems calling for help rather than retribution.

It is true that as criminal and delinquent behavior increase, the "sickness" view of bad behavior is coming under criticism. Yet the basis of the criticism is still pragmatic—that the more humane approach does not seem to work. Presumably more severe measures would. But so long as we damn a humane approach because it doesn't work, we are still calling for better treatment rather than for punishment, by whatever the name we call it. Cancer, we are saying, needs drastic surgery rather than a few vitamins. Yet both surgery and taking vitamins are still forms of treatment.

Punishment on the other hand implies moral wrongdoing. It is not given because it is effective but because justice demands that it be given, whatever the outcome may prove to be. The rise in crime, then, might merely reflect a need for more powerful treatment of criminals and not for retribution. Treatment (discipline) and punishment are justified by different criteria. The acid question in the case of punishment is, Is it just? People are punished even though there is no guarantee that punishment will change them.

Let me be clear. The value of discipline and/or treatment is unquestioned. It is biblical. It has the support both of traditional wisdom and of science. What I oppose is the divorce of punishment from discipline and the rejection of the former. I firmly recommend that we both discipline and punish. I maintain that our unthinking tendency to emphasize discipline at the expense of punishment and to think of the measures we adopt primarily in terms of their effect on the disciplined person is both unchristian and morally dangerous. Far from being humane it opens the way to worse tyranny both in society and in the home than punishment ever will. It leads to logical confusion, is at variance with Scripture and adds to rather than alleviates parental burdens.

A Society without Mercy

I imagine many Christians are as uneasy as I myself am at our rejection of a punishment model in favor of a treatment model. Other Christians are caught up with the modern mood, even when they think of God. They prefer to see his actions as disciplinary, designed only to train and correct his people, but grow uneasy when you talk of a punishing God who visits people with judgment.

But we cannot get rid of punishment without getting rid automatically of things we all value highly. If we reject punishment (with the associated idea that punishment is *deserved* or *merited* and that God acts justly when he punishes), then we are left with a mere Heavenly Technician giving treatment. The Judge is no more. In that case we must stop talking about his mercy and forgiveness. As C. S. Lewis points out, "If crime is only a disease which needs a cure, not a sin which deserves punishment, it cannot be pardoned. How can you pardon a man for having a gumboil or a clubfoot?" If God were only a technician, he still might be kind enough to give us all treatment. But he would not be able to bestow the sovereign grace only a holy God can give sinners.

Let us look for a moment at some social consequences of treating criminals before we consider the consequences for family life. In California a treatment approach to crime has been in effect for some years. Offenders there are given indeterminate sentences (let us say between two and ten years) for particular offenses.

Under the California system the length of the offenders' sentences depends on how well they respond to treatment. Before the system came into effect good behavior would *merit* early release. It was a credit to the prisoners. But under the present system an expert treating prisoners may view such behavior as cover-ups for unresolved emotional problems that the offenders, sometimes viewed by their therapists as con artists, are trying to hide. Thus only an expert can assess whether the criminal is getting better. A psychologist or a social worker must feel the prisoner's emotional pulse with sensitive fingers to assess his or her progress.

From the criminals' point of view it is eminently unsatisfactory. An entirely new principle has been introduced against which they have no appeal if there is any injustice. Under the old system they knew what to expect when sentenced to ten years in jail. The worst that could happen was that they would spend ten years of imprisoned misery. After that they had a right to go free.

Under the new system these moral invalids do have some protection. A maximum length of treatment is prescribed. If therapy fails after the ten-year maximum, they are released from prison. But during this time in jail they never know how long they will be treated since their length of stay does not depend on a precise sentence with the chance of meriting an early release according to criteria fully understood by the prisoners, by the guards and by the warden. Rather it depends on the judgment of an expert on human behavior as to psychological processes alleged to be taking place in their minds.

The criminals do not see what they get as treatment. To them, whatever anyone else says, it is punishment. It is a new and terrible form of punishment, and they have no means of knowing how long it will go on. It is kindness they did not ask for, kindness that is forced on them until someone decides they have had enough.

The situation is worse in some experimental treatment centers in the West where no limits are set on the length of treatment. The other day I came across documents describing a review of a black man of thirty-seven who had been held in such a treatment center against his will for twenty years. He had been referred there after stealing a car for a joy ride. He was judged by the psychologist at the center to be hostile, aggressive and dangerous though he had not committed any hostile or dangerous acts and was not mentally ill in any sense. He had, however, consistently displayed a hostile attitude in the treatment center, complaining that he had been imprisoned for twenty years for an offense for which his former friends had merely been fined a small sum of money.

I am sure the psychologist in question can give convincing reasons for his views, but the logical consequences of adopting a discipline/treatment outlook on unwanted behavior while abandoning the idea of "just deserts" means there is no built-in protection for prisoners. Their rights are not considered. What at first may seem kind and humane becomes in practice a nightmare of tyranny—even in the hands of well-disposed and kindly persons honestly trying to help.

May God defend us from tyrannical kindness! Mercy detached from justice, as Lewis points out, grows unmerciful.

If the tyranny of unwanted kindness can produce such terrible injustice, what will the consequences be if the treatment model is adopted by ill-disposed and wicked governments? George Orwell warned us what might happen in his novel *1984* and news from Russia suggests he was an accurate prophet.

Justice in the Home

If you opt for a discipline/treatment model at home, the consequences are also destructive. Most parents rarely think of the distinction between discipline and punishment but rightly view a given measure both as discipline ("it will teach him a lesson") and punishment ("he had it coming to him"). Yet since the child-rearing books deal exclusively with discipline and give no guidance about punishment other than that we abandon it, then the more we read them the more concerned we grow about the results of the way we handle our children and the less concerned with the justice of what we do.

We parents stand in the place of God in our families. Unlike God, we sin. Unlike God, we make mistakes. Nevertheless within the limitations of our fallible judgments we can, like God, be just. Our children need justice if they are to grow up with a sense that the universe is founded on a righteous basis. The universe is not an amoral laboratory conditioning us to appropriate social behavior. More important, children have a right to justice. They have in fact a sensitive (though not always accurate) idea of it and keenly resent injustice. Therefore we must give them justice as well as help.

To focus on the results of our discipline is to focus on the problem rather than the children. And to focus on the problem is in some measure to dehumanize the children. In their obsession with a problem some parents get into power struggles which in theory ought never to occur. The eradication of a bad trait or the establishment of a good one by applying a scientific principle should require nothing more than patience and consistency. But when the bad trait fails to disappear parents sometimes grit their teeth and determine to hang on. Perspective is lost and the struggle that develops can be ugly. If the method selected involves physical chastisement, parents find themselves shrinking increasingly from the ordeal of inflicting repeated pain on a shocked, bewildered and uncomprehending child. Despair and alienation may be the final result.

The failure and the frustration may have nothing to do with the method selected but arise from the false perspective. Children who can always be conditioned are not children but robots. Child behavior cannot always be shaped by behavioral engineering and attempts to do so will sometimes lead to an impasse.

I remember a father who had reached such an impasse with his seventeen-year-old son who had a weakness for stealing. One day when there was incontrovertible evidence that the boy had been trying to break into his sister's bedroom window, the father's despair and inner rage overwhelmed him.

"I told God I hated him [God]. I told him I could take no more. I asked him either to kill me or to kill the boy—I'd really reached the limit. I'd done everything I could, disciplined firmly and consistently, been understanding, established a good rapport with the boy. For years I'd put up with court appearances, family therapy from psychiatrists, crisis after crisis. He'd been O.K. for weeks. Then this. I don't know what happened to me or why I reacted so strongly, but inside me all hell broke loose. I didn't have anything left.

"Then it dawned on me that in my discipline I was always trying to control something in Bob's life. It had never occurred to me to punish him because justice demanded punishment—whether what I did controlled his stealing or not. I felt scared because at that point I knew it would have to mean a stick on his rear end, and all the books advised against corporal punishment, especially for kids of his age. Besides, he's heavier and stronger than me. I knew a fight would be a disaster.

"I prayed about it for hours. It was the only course I had peace about. He accepted it like a lamb when I explained he had to be punished for doing evil, and he opened up like he's never opened up before. Something happened, I can't put my finger on it. It had nothing to do with the physical part but the simple business of coming to terms with justice. He's never been the same since."

Ironically, though no result was being sought, results actually followed. But just as remarkable as the change in the boy, was the resolution of the father's agony. From frustration and despair he had found peace. Pressed for an explanation he wrinkled his forehead. "It had something to do with not being responsible anymore for the results of what I did. Up to then I felt *I* was failing—and maybe I was. But it was more than that, it was just that what I was doing was so right.... "

Was it right?

I am not discussing physical punishment but the whole idea of punishment, whatever the nature of the sentence. I am certainly not discussing brutality, vengefulness, vindictiveness or any attempt by parents to take their bitterness out on children. Rather I am asking whether it is morally right to inflict a penalty on children primarily in the interests of justice and not merely as a matter of training; that is, because they deserve it and not merely to teach them a lesson.

The Dignity in Punishment

B. F. Skinner both in fiction and expository prose has boldly outlined a scheme to bring about a world order of peace by using what I have called the treatment model. Skinner does not see people as made in the image of God. Indeed one of his books is entitled *Beyond Human Dignity*. Without thinking, many Christians have opted for a Skinnerian approach to child raising. Because they are Christians, they subscribe theoretically to the idea of human dignity, of the dignity of their children, but fail to see the inconsistency between their faith and their child-rearing methods. Yet in divorcing discipline from punishment they join forces with Skinner. Such parents shape behavior patterns, exterminating undesirable traits, conditioning and deconditioning. The more closely they follow certain child-rearing manuals (be those manuals "Christian" or not), the more they become concerned with the "end product," a convenient "end product" that will fit more comfortably into family life, church life and society in general.

They have unwittingly fallen into error. They have ruled out mercy and have adopted principles inimical to human dignity. Skinner freely recognizes this. You cannot mold someone's character and behavior without regarding that someone as a *something*. You have gone beyond human dignity into a Skinnerian world.

You may have also been placing as your highest goal the quality of conformity and entered Skinner's world without knowing it. Do you say to yourself, "How can I make my children fit into our family? Into church? Into society? Will they be comfortable to live with? Will they have enough initiative to be a leader, a leader who will lead people along paths tried and true?" For you do not want to raise prophets or reformers! Nor let loose on the world children who think, decide and feel for themselves!

Happily our children resist our best efforts to fit them into molds. They wriggle and they struggle until the behavioral molds crack and splinter. They may not know what dignity is, but its presence in them cries out to be heard. The dignity that God placed there will defy our attempts until we are compelled to see the image of God in the little ones we try to shape to our pleasure.

Few divine attributes move us more than a display of God's

mercy. Mercy awakens awe in us. It awakens our desire to worship and appeals to that which is most noble in our characters. It can have the same effect on our children.

Training and discipline alone do not allow for mercy. It is not merciful of a dentist to ignore a decayed tooth and send a child home. It is not merciful of a coach to excuse a top athlete from a critical part of training. In the same way, to adopt exclusively a therapeutic approach to child rearing rules out the practice of mercy as well as of punishment.

"I am going to show you mercy," said a magistrate to an offender who well knew his guilt and who had anticipated a severe sentence. The magistrate evidently knew what he was doing for the amazed offender was never again seen in court and led an exemplary life. Yet it is not for that reason I mention the matter, but because only within the framework of right, wrong, punishment and retribution is there any room for the idea of mercy.

How shall our children learn mercy unless it is shown to them? How shall they learn that wrong deserves punishment unless they are not only disciplined but punished? How shall we as parents accord our children the dignity of true humanity unless we teach them that their moral wrong merits punishment and that punishment in some ways rights the wrong they have committed? How shall we teach them the sinfulness of sin if we treat it as a bad habit we can train them out of? Punishment may teach a child to quit sinning, but it should be given if it is truly merited whether it will make the child quit or not. And in considering whether a child deserves punishment we shall hopefully think long and hard before deciding on a just sentence.

Yet I suspect our children really do not need to be taught that sin is sinful. They already know. It is we, their parents, who have frustrated ourselves and added to our pain by struggling vainly to shape bad behavior, having failed to see it as sin that called for either retribution or grace.

It is not beyond dignity we are called to move, but out of the shallows of a sterile pragmatism into the dignity of the imageo Dei.

The Punishment of Expulsion

We must deal with our children as God has dealt with us. Having enunciated this principle and having looked at the judicial concept of punishment, I cannot leave these ideas without following them to their logical conclusions.

God's judgment on erring Israel eventually meant the disappearance of the northern kingdom and the enslavement of the southern kingdom for seventy years. If we deal with our children as God dealt with his ancient people, what might be our own sentence on their persistent rebellion? God gives us the dignity of choice. Should parents do the same? Does there come a time when parents should oblige their children to leave the home because of their sin?

God was long-suffering with Israel and Judah. He warned, he chastised and during hundreds of years he waited. He had spelled out the details of his covenant with them through Moses even before Israel was a nation. His prophets repeatedly pointed to the covenant as well as to Israel's sins. From time to time through defeat in war, through famine and disaster God visited them with discipline. His warnings of their approaching doom eventually became more and more specific.

In the end God allowed his people to reap what they had sown. The northern kingdom went into captivity and has disappeared from the face of the earth. Judah also was ravaged and its inhabitants taken north from whence many years later only a remnant returned home.

An identical pattern emerges in the New Testament. We see the long-suffering of Jesus in the parable of the fig tree (Lk. 13:6-9). Judgment must ultimately come, but every opportunity will first be given for repentance. Jesus exemplified the principle in his own attitude both to individuals and churches. Speaking of "the woman Jezebel," Jesus says, "I gave her time to repent, but she refuses to repent of her immorality. Behold, I will throw her on a sickbed" (Rev. 2:21-22). Again, addressing the church at Sardis he says, "Remember then what you received and heard; keep that, and repent. If you will not awake, I will come like a thief" (Rev. 3:3).

God's dealings with his people form a pattern for Christian parents. Like him we may eventually have to allow our persistently rebellious children to harvest the consequences of their willfulness. The time can come when we have to withdraw all support from them and oblige them, because of their own decisions, to leave home. Under what circumstances should so painful a decision be made? What are the guidelines for expelling a rebellious youngster from the house?

Clearly children should not be thrown out in a fit of petulant rage. Our home has at times served as a temporary refuge for young people (ranging in age from thirteen to seventeen) who have been ordered out of their own homes during a family fight. "Get out! Get out of this house! And don't you ever show your face round here again!" is a common wording for the dismissal. In most cases the teen-agers are back home again within a month or so, grudgingly tolerated until the next blowup. But sometimes the dismissal sticks.

Joe and Allison had a sixteen-year-old boy named David who wound up in juvenile court with a charge of stealing a truck, taking it on a joy ride round the city, sideswiping two cars and careening into a lamppost. David and two friends were not hurt. Nor were the people in the sideswiped cars. But David had been drinking, and this was the third time he had combined drinking and joy-riding.

Allison lost several nights' sleep. Was it her fault? She could think of some areas of failure. Because she worked as a social worker, she had not always been at home when the children needed her. On the other hand she had encouraged all three of her children in sports (at which they excelled). She had attended David's school matches and his club matches. She had also paid for extra coaching in view of his obvious talent. Had she pushed him too much at football? She didn't think so. She was proud of him, naturally, but she didn't think his successes were the result of any ego trip on her part.

She felt added shame in that her work mainly consisted of family counseling. She was supposed to be an expert in these matters. And now David.... To whom could she turn for help? She was ashamed to go to her colleagues. And when she thought of her own priest (she was a Roman Catholic), she snorted contemptuously. On the other hand there was Father Duval. But Father Duval was away from his own parish just then.

Joe's reaction was violent. "Out he goes! We've already given him too many chances. We've been soft on the little brat. It's time he learned his lesson." Joe worked in construction as a foreman.

He and David quarreled violently, one of many quarrels that had increased in intensity as David's delinquencies mounted. Joe was indifferent to the fact that they were both legally responsible for any more damage David might do. ("I'm paying out *no more* money. Get it? I don't care what the court says. I'll go to jail, see? I don't give a damn!") He was too angry to share Allison's feeling that David was not mature enough to take care of himself. ("If he can drive a truck round town and smash cars up, then he's old enough to work for a living and to look after himself. To hell with him.")

Allison, too, was angry—angry not only with Joe but with David. But she was a mother and her protective feelings had the upper hand during their quarrel. Moreover, as a social worker she recognized their legal position. She also knew from the inside what the various youth centers and rehabilitative centers in the city were like. She could refer clients to them, but she would never send David. So she pleaded with Joe.

Two months later David disappeared after a row with his father in which Joe had told him to "get lost for good." Allison told me she just had to accept the fact that she had done all she could and that David had to be allowed to make his own choices. Moreover her relationship with Joe was important. She wasn't going to throw it away because of David.

"I can't just stop living because of this. It could get me down if I let it. But I've quit letting it bother me."

"And Joe?"

"Oh, Joe seems to have forgotten all about it. If it comes up he just says, 'Well, good luck to the little brat wherever he is.'" She smiled and shrugged. She was still a warm person and very likable. But over the previous year she had toughened and become harder. She had had no help, professional or religious.

I have seen at least a couple of letters in Ann Landers's column during the last year or so recounting a happy ending to the story of a boy or girl who had been thrown out of the house. The teen-ager turned up after a year or so, respectably dressed, steadily employed, attitude transformed. To experience the hard knocks of the world firsthand was enough to "straighten them out." Some people use such examples as an argument in favor of expulsion. But many questions remain in a parent's mind. Will it really work or will my child only go more deeply into the mire? More important, is it right? Is it just? Is it what God would want?

The decision can be painful. One father of an erring daughter told me, "I combed the beaches for her that day. I had prayed, 'Lord, if I can't find her today I am at an end. I can't go on helping her forever.' I didn't find her. I stuck to that since. She had put herself outside the area of our being able to help her. We loved her still. . . . "

Some parents are too tortured by self-doubt to act decisively. A father of a twenty-year-old wrote me, "I have contemplated sending my daughter away, but I realize this is no solution, only selfishness. Somehow I must love her; and as long as she wants to stay with us, I believe . . . I should permit her to. I need to talk with her and let her know I don't understand her lifestyle, and yet I must not do this unless I can do it in love. . . . I have contemplated quitting my job and moving and making a home [elsewhere] for her."

There are times when an explosive situation demands fast action. Bitterness often rises in the "good" children whom the parents may neglect in their desire to restore their prodigal to his or her senses. And sometimes matters go so far that the parents are forced to choose whom they would rather have at home, the problem child or the nonproblem children. The squeaky wheel may get so much grease that the silent wheels disconnect themselves from the axle and roll away.

Parents who are reluctant to take drastic steps should ask themselves why. Are they too scared? There is every reason to be scared. What parent is not? The thought of exposing a child to physical hardship, to loneliness and to moral temptation flies in the face of every parental instinct. Or is it that parents fear public opinion? Are they still clinging to unrealistic hopes that matters will magically right themselves if only they hang on a little longer when it is plain they will not?

Parents who cling to their erring children must realize that by paying debts and legal expenses beyond clearly set guidelines, or even by offering continued shelter, food and clothing, they can morally become a party to the delinquent behavior. Their actions can make it possible for rebellious children to continue to live as they have in the past. Home for them is merely a free hotel. Instead of helping them to follow godliness, parents are giving their children the message that there is no need for them to be godly since they, their parents, will always look after them and get them out of a hole.

The decision to dismiss children from home should not be made either because it will work or as a matter of expediency. It should be made on the basis of justice. And justice must consider every side of the problem. Is it morally just to keep children at home when other family members suffer deprivation in one form or another because of them? Are they old enough to care for themselves, that is, to hunt for work and provide themselves with food and shelter? Are they of legal age? Have they had plenty of warning about what will happen if they continue in the same way? Have the warnings been merely angry threats or serious talks explaining why such a measure should be adopted? Has a deadline been set of which they are well aware? Has the matter of visiting rights been thought out? How often may they come home for meals? Should they ever stay the night? Or should we avoid the thin end of the wedge until and unless the sow has abandoned the mire?

I do not have answers to all the questions I raise, but I must answer some. Clearly parents must not only think through the problems of separation well in advance, but must also discuss them in detail with the children concerned. Three critical areas must be included: visiting privileges, finances and a deadline. In addition to all these, the logistics of the actual move should be discussed. All will tend to make children more aware of the reality of the step.

In my judgment visits home should be encouraged unless strong reasons to the contrary exist. An occasional evening meal and a visit home every Sunday may be a good arrangement. Such visits will enable the parents to counsel children and to learn what kind of improvement has been made that might make reinstatement possible. The expulsion is punishment enough without total abandonment.

Finances must also be discussed for the reasons I have already given. If the children are unemployed, parents will naturally be anxious. Yet unemployment alone is not sufficient grounds to keep youngsters at home. It may be painful for them to have to hunt for work and to apply for welfare for interim support, but the very pain may be salutary, forcing children to face the reality of the struggle for survival. Handouts from parents will defeat the object of the expulsion.

The age at which an erring child will be required to leave home will be critical in deciding a deadline. It would be wrong to expel children who are too young to care for themselves. Parents must exercise careful judgment about children's preparedness. Children mature at different rates. Many are on their own by the time they are sixteen.

God had his own deadline for Israel and Judah. And when the time came he acted in judgment and righteousness. He still made it clear that their repentance would mean that he would bring them back. But for the present they must suffer the withdrawal of his favor and his support.

How are we to view God's terrible judgment on his people, especially on the vanished Israelites from the northern kingdom? We know that he is not a cold and inscrutable judge. However exact his judgments, he remains a God of love.

Yet love must respect the dignity, the personhood of the beloved. You cannot love someone truly and deny that person the dignity of facing the results of his or her decisions. To do anything else would be to betray true love for something less than love, a "love" tainted by selfishness and weakness. Paradoxically we cannot love unless we risk the doom of the one we love.

God respected the dignity of our primal forefathers. He could have prevented their tragic disobedience and could thus have circumvented all the tragedies of human existence. He gave them a choice. They chose rebellion. He was then obliged to drive them from the garden.

If God so respects the autonomy he gave us, then we also must do the same for our children. In their earliest years they are not ready to be given full control of their lives because they are too vulnerable, too weak, too inexperienced to use it. But when the time comes, and that time must be decided by the parents as they wait on God, we must give them the dignity of letting them face the real consequences of their actions.

To do so will be painful. If ever you find yourself in that position, beware of sealing your heart in bitterness. The test of godly maturity will be to carry out the sentence combining tenderness with firmness. You need not say the words to your child, but in your heart like Samuel you must say, "Far be it from me that I should sin against the LORD by ceasing to pray for you" (1 Sam. 12:23).

12
The Model Parent

*I*f you were dissatisfied with the loaves-and-fishes principle of parenting in chapter ten, you had good reason to be. It is too diffuse, too lacking in substance to be adequate. We need clear goals to strive for. There are times without number when a parent cries in desperation, "What *ought* I to do? How *should* I react?" The loaves-and-fishes principle will be a clearing of the ground, a beginning, a facing of the enormous gap between what we are as parents and what we should be; in a word, between ourselves and God.

A Parent in God's Image

Let me restate the basic rule of parenting: As God is to me so must I be to my children. As he has dealt with me, so must I deal with them. Such kindness as he has shown me, such patience and forbearing, such intolerance of sin—these must I in turn show to those for whom I stand in place of God. For in my children's minds a concept of God is growing which is derived from my spouse and me, two powerful beings who gave them birth and who seem to rule over the cosmos of the home.

Each time my children see a godlike attitude or action in their father or mother, the Holy Spirit will tell them, "Now you can understand a little better what your Father in heaven is like."

Yet our striving to this higher goal must not be merely for our children's sake. Just as we are called to be holy because God is holy, so we are called to be parents because he is a parent, and that is reason enough. We were created in his image and to that image, even the image of God the Parent, we are called to be faithful.

"For this reason I bow my knees before the Father, from whom every family in heaven and on earth is named, . . . " Paul wrote to Christians in Ephesus nineteen centuries ago (3:14-15). What was he saying? He was saying that the family is a divine institution which arises in God's very being and from God's essential nature. Francis Foulkes writes, "The apostle is saying, think of any 'father-headed group' in heaven and earth. Each one is named from him. From him it derives its existence and its concept and experience of fatherhood. As Severian . . . puts it, 'The name of father did not go up from us, but from above came to us.' "[1]

He is our parent. From his very being our parental instincts spring. The commonest name by which Jesus refers to God is Father, yet the idea that God is Father does not arise for the first time in the New Testament. He is the "father of the fatherless" (Ps. 68:5). "As a father pities his children," David sang, "so the LORD pities those who fear him. For he knows our frame; he remembers that we are dust" (Ps. 103:13-14). Moreover, parenthood is not merely an attribute of the first person of the Godhead but of the triune God. "Everlasting Father" is a name given to the coming Messiah (Is. 9:6). "For I am a father to Israel," says Yahweh through Jeremiah's lips, "and Ephraim is my first-born" (31:9).

What more moving understanding could there be of God as Father than the graphic picture painted by Jesus of the man who was awaiting the return of the prodigal son? Here is a father who allows his son to leave him, knowing full well all that is to befall him. It is a father who stands on the roof of his house, straining his keen eyes to where the dusty road blurs into the horizon.

For how many months or years does he go on watching? How many times does he start eagerly as another distant figure approaches only to let his shoulders drop in disappointment as he perceives his hopes are vain? Yet there comes a day when his pulse begins to race and his legs to shake, and with a shout he stumbles down the stairway, running through the gate like a madman and calling to his servants to follow him. His legs eat up the yards between father and son and with a cry of joy he flings himself at his boy.

This, Jesus explains to a critical crowd, is how God relates to repentant sinners—as a father to a dearly loved son. This ecstasy, this ravishing joy, these shouted orders for the best robe, the ring and the merriment of a feast are to help us understand not only that God is father but what manner of father he is.

"What father among you," Jesus once asked his listeners, "if his son asks for a fish, will instead of a fish give him a serpent; or if he asks for an egg, will give him a scorpion? If you then, who are evil, know how to give good gifts to your children, how much more will the heavenly Father give the Holy Spirit to those who ask him!" (Lk. 11:11-13).

The fatherhood principle goes further yet. "Abba, Father" the Son of man cried in a moment of deep perplexity (Mk. 14:36). Abba is said by some commentators to be equivalent to "daddy" or "dad" in English, though perhaps a more restrained "my own father" would be better. The awesome God of creation is addressed by Jesus with a term that a child uses confidently. The child has no thought of disrespect. "My father" is what the father has taught the child to call him. "My father" is the name that he or she alone may use. Friends and neighbors are limited to other forms of address.

And we, as fellow heirs of Christ Jesus are also instructed of the Spirit to call him "Abba" (Rom. 8:15). If we are but willing to take the place of little children before him, we may know the same privilege. For the expression "my father" is one of privilege more than of intimacy, the privilege of claiming the loving protection that the child claims of the great being from whom he has sprung.

God is not merely *like* a father. If we could distill every human idea of fatherhood into a concentrated essence, we would have but a faint reflection of his fatherliness. He is a better parent than any of us will ever be.

You will notice that I have been using the words *father* and *parent* interchangeably. I do so for a reason. Where could mother qualities come from if they did not come from God? And woman is also, no less than man, made in the image of God (Gen. 1:27).

Whatever may be the reason for referring to God as "he" and for referring to his parental relationship with us as father, rather than as mother, it certainly is not to suggest that no motherly qualities are there or that they are somehow less important.

"Like an eagle that stirs up its nest," sang Moses "that flutters over its young, spreading out its wings, catching them, bearing them on its pinions, the LORD alone did lead him . . . " (Deut. 32:11-12). God's care for Israel was like the mother eagle's care for her young.

"O Jerusalem, Jerusalem," cried Jesus, "killing the prophets and stoning those who are sent to you! How often would I have gathered your children together as a hen gathers her brood under her wings" (Lk. 13:34). Jesus felt about the inhabitants of Jerusalem as a mother hen feels about her threatened chicks.

The picture becomes more explicit in Isaiah. "You shall suck, you shall be carried upon her hip, and dandled upon her knees. As one whom his mother comforts, so I will comfort you" Yahweh tells Jerusalem (Is. 66:12-13). "Can a woman forget her sucking child, that she should have no compassion on the son of her womb?" he asks, and continues, "Even these may forget, yet I will not forget you" (Is. 49:15).

Some differences between male and female parents arise from culture and custom while others are innate, inborn. But God is the source of them all, innate or culturebound. He is not father in the sense of not being mother. He can accurately be referred to as father-mother God. He is the source of all that is truly motherly and truly fatherly, and we are all, both fathers and mothers, called to be like him.

The God of the Covenants
He is the God of the covenants. Covenants were binding contract agreements between two parties. But God's covenants with his people were not negotiated between him and them. His people took no part in defining the terms of the covenants. Instead God decided what the contents were to be and then bestowed them on his people, pledging his own commitment both to the people and to his covenant with them. They were agreements defining the privileges and blessings of God's people and their relationship to him. His people's part was by faith to accept or in unbelief and rebellion to reject his covenants, to be bound by them or to rebel against them.

We do not consciously confer covenants on our children, yet in a way our relationship with them is similar to God's with his people. Like him, we initiate the style of the relationship, deciding what it will be. Our children may dislike and rebel against it or wish that the contents of the unspoken covenant were different, but for better or worse we, like God, bestow a relationship on the children God has given us. By and large we commit ourselves to it, governing ourselves by its unspoken, unwritten clauses. We do not question the fact that we must feed, clothe and shelter our children as we prepare them for the task of living independently in the world. The covenant may never arise in our consciousness, but it is there and we bind ourselves to fulfill it.

God's covenants were conditional. "If you obey the voice of the LORD your God," Moses told Israel, "being careful to do all his commandments . . . all these blessings shall come upon you and overtake you, if you obey the voice of the LORD your God" (Deut. 28:1-2). God would not tolerate sin. He might be long-suffering. Certainly he understood the frailty of our fallen nature and tempered his judgments with patience and mercy. But in his plan to provide a way of salvation for humanity, there could be no compromise on the issues of rebellion, disobedience and sin. The covenant relationship was to be on his terms. He was holy and the relationship was to be a holy one. Indeed its very purpose was to deliver us all from sin and draw us back to holiness.

And the holiness was to be absolute holiness. Not a hair's breadth must his people deviate from his ways. In a vision Amos saw a plumb line, symbolizing the absolute standard God demanded of his people (Amos 7:7). And if God makes such demands of us, ought we not also to make those same demands of our children? Yet the standard is impossible for them. Moreover, how dare we demand holiness of our children when we ourselves are weak and rebellious? How indeed? But the standard is there, and we are called to attain it and to demand it.

The God of the covenant is, however, a God of mercy. "He does not deal with us according to our sins, nor requite us according to our iniquities" (Ps. 103:10). Knowing our weakness and pitying it, loving us with an everlasting love, he found a way to come to terms with the dilemma. Blood could be shed and sin could be forsaken.

But what have I said? Have I said that God demands perfection and yet at the same time does not demand it? That he warns against the consequences of sin yet fails to keep his word and weakly excuses it? That his demand for obedience is hollow so that we need not be too concerned about our lapses from moral perfection? By no means.

There is but one standard and that standard is God himself. We are called to be holy because he is. We are called to be as holy as he. God permits no excuses. Mercy and laxity are not the same thing. God does not excuse our sin. In his mercy he pays for it, redeems us from it, making of Christ the propitiation for it. However terrible the price, there could be and there will be no compromise on the issue of sin.

How then shall we as parents reflect God's attitude about sin to our children? First, we must teach them what sin is. By our actions, by our words, by the demands we place on them we must teach them the difference between right and wrong, between truth and lying, between sin and holiness. They may eventually reject the teaching, but that is their affair. Our responsibility is to give it.

And we must do more. We must show them that sin must be paid for. It cannot merely be excused nor can we pretend it does not exist. We must teach them both by disciplining them and by punishing them. We must point out that even though at times we may show mercy, the cost of sin somehow, somewhere has to be met. We may perhaps on one occasion forgive the angry smashing of an object. But we must show how suffering and inconvenience will be the price paid by others for the mercy we have shown.

It goes without saying that we must teach them by our example, yet how will this be possible when our example is so poor? It is here we despair because we do not understand the nature of the example we are called to give. We may not be perfect, but we can refuse to excuse our imperfection. God does not want us to impress our children with our spiritual success so much as to let them see that we take his demands seriously for ourselves. We should freely acknowledge our failings and confess our sins when we have wronged our children. But we must still strive to fulfill Christ's law.

Above all we must point to the sacrifice of Christ both in relation to our own sins and those of our children. One youth I heard about received a drastic lesson on the cost of mercy when the elders of a local church decreed that the boy be present to watch his own father physically beaten for offenses the youth had committed. It was a lesson the boy never forgot. I do not recommend the practice as a standard procedure, but we must collaborate with the Holy Spirit in teaching our children the costliness of sin and of the mercy that forgives it.

It is at this point that many of us have been so superficial. We regarded correction merely as a means to an end, the production of desirable character. Our goal must be far more profound. As parents we must teach our children the sinfulness of sin and the terrible price of mercy. Let those who will, criticize our outmoded "puritanical" stance. We stand in the place of God to our children. We must not merely aim at molding them to please us. We are to be faithful to our charge of accurately representing the greatest Father of all in his attitude toward sin.

The God of Compassion

God is not only merciful, he is compassionate and understanding. "As a father pities his children, so the LORD pities those who fear him. For he knows our frame; he remembers that we are dust" (Ps. 103:13-14). He knows. He remembers. He is aware of our feelings, our weaknesses, our inadequacies, and knowing them he enters into our experience and sympathizes. He is under no obligation to do so save for an obligation to his own nature. He would not be true to himself were he not to enter into our experience with compassionate understanding. In this capacity he is also acting as a parent. We may count on that understanding for it is always present.

But upon our shoulders rests an equal burden. Because we are understood, we must understand. Because we are pitied, we must pity. The measure of compassion we receive must be the measure of compassion we give.

To have compassion is not the same as to be easygoing. Some of us give way to our children's wishes from laziness. We do not wish to go to the trouble of assessing how appropriate a request may be. Or we are reluctant to face our children's resentment either by refusing their request or by our exercise of discipline. We are soft. We give in. And in doing so we occasionally fool ourselves into believing that we are being compassionate when we are merely being weak kneed.

Compassion gets along excellently with firmness. Firmness says, "Thus shall it be!" while compassion adds, "Thus indeed it may have to be, but I must enter into my children's feelings. I must not deepen their despair by my coldness nor add to their burdens by my indifference. I must temper judgment with mercy, strictness with concern."

To do so will at times cost us dearly. It is precisely on those days when our children have most need of compassionate understanding that we ourselves are too hurt to care for anything but our own pain. "How many more times?" we ask in despair, feeling that our store of compassion has long since been exhausted, that we cannot draw water when our wells are dry.

Yet we have a Father whose compassions never fail but are renewed morning by morning. To him we ourselves must turn and drink compassion until our thirst is quenched, allowing his inexhaustible fountains, his endlessly gushing springs of compassion to wash over and through us. We must think about the compassion he has toward us, thanking and praising him for it whether we feel it or not. For it is real. It flows over us even when we least perceive it. In thanking him our own dry wells will fill again. As Mary Shekleton writes,

I am an empty vessel—not one thought
Or look of love I ever to Thee brought;
Yet I may come, and come again to Thee
With this, the empty sinner's only plea—
    Thou lovest me.[2]

Yet whether we feel compassion or not, even though we may not perceive how freely and fully it flows to us, we must adopt an attitude of compassionate understanding to our children. We owe it to our heavenly Father to do so. Our rebellious wills may not be easy to tame, and we may have to allow time for the flames of our resentment to burn out. But do so we must and can. For compassion is not a feeling but an attitude of our wills, an attitude we can choose to adopt however reluctant we may feel about doing so.

You might argue, telling me that the very word *compassion* means "to feel with" our children. Possibly so. But I refuse to play word games. There is an attitude I can adopt toward my children. My feelings may not be in the least compassionate. But I can defy my feelings. I have a will, a will that can overrule my pettiness and hurt so that I force myself to look at my children, force myself to remember what it was like to be a child, force myself to consider how difficult it must be for them to control their feelings and actions, force myself to remember how I have been tempted also and how difficult I found temptation to resist.

Feelings of compassion may follow and probably will. But if I were to wait for them to occur naturally before showing compassion, the feelings might never come and my children would be the victims of my moods. Our Father is no whimsical Father, and we must learn to be like him. If the attitude we deliberately adopt is one of compassion, then our actions and words will reveal compassion.

The Prodigal Released

The father of the prodigal son let his son go. And God the Father of us all does likewise. He who could coerce our wills refuses to. There is a limit even to his pleading. He does not block the doorway as we try to leave him, flooding us with a thousand arguments. Nor does he pursue us pestering us with, "I told you so." He gives us the full dignity of choice.

There is wisdom as well as justice in what he fails to do. There are times when our wills are so set on disastrous courses that disaster alone will teach us. There is nothing like a belly full of husks to teach a man that he's a fool.

But as parents we are selfish in our loves. We cannot let go We refuse to see what stares us in the face, that a heart set o' folly will not be dissuaded by reason.

Habits are hard to break. "She just *will not* learn," we tell ourselves in frustration, having gone over the lesson with an obstinate daughter for the hundredth time. The habit of correcting her has grown to be so much a part of us. As the time draws closer for her to live her own life, we correct her all the more fiercely. We are scared by what we see awaiting her. And in our terror we become the more diligent to avert tragedy and attempt to teach the unheeded lesson for the hundred-and-first time. We cannot believe our own words, that she just will *not* learn! For she just won't.

It is not love that makes us so persistent, but fear. The time has come for relinquishment, and we lack both the love for our child and the trust in God to relinquish the battle of wills. Growth into adulthood demands the continual exercise of choice. In adolescent years our children vacillate between an innate drive to become independent from us and the habit of childhood to cling to us dependently. The nearer they get to adulthood, the greater becomes the drive for independence. And independence implies learning to trust one's own judgment. You cannot make real choices without running real perils. And we cannot defend our children from the perils of their own choices.

Again and again I have listened to sadder but wiser parents say to me, "I had to realize that it was his life and hold my tongue. I just kept myself available."

Do not feel guilty about allowing your children to reap what they have sown for this is how God deals with all of us. He does not enjoy letting us pursue our stubborn way until we live with pigs, but faced with a choice between giving us the full dignity of personhood with all its attendant risks or enslaving us to involuntary servitude like the beasts, he chooses the former. He could not make us a little lower than the angels without facing the possibility that we might choose to become little better than demons. Love says, "I will give you the high dignity of choice, even though you choose to fling my gift back in my face."

Clearly, letting go is a matter of degree, and the degree to which I let go will increase over the years. In fact our hand may often be forced by realities which wrest control from us. Yet if we adopt an attitude of relinquishment, we may save ourselves and our children some needless frustration. Moreover, we will be giving our children the same high dignity that God gives us.

All is not lost when our children make foolish choices. It will be painful for us to watch them eat hog's food, but there is hope that when that happens they will learn from experience what they never could have learned from precept.

Justice Comes Down

Our Father in heaven is just. His response to our sin is appropriate. It is never excessive and never reflects his petulance. Moreover, he has always gone to the trouble of finding out exactly what the situation was in which we sinned. He relies neither on angelic gossip nor on demonic tattling.

"I have seen the affliction of my people who are in Egypt, and have heard their cry because of their taskmasters; I know their sufferings" (Ex. 3:7). God had seen, had heard and knew for himself. Again, before he inflicts doom on Sodom we hear him say, "I will go down to see whether they have done altogether according to the outcry which has come to me; and if not, I will know" (Gen. 18:21). God's omniscience is not a passive status quo but is active.

He has always been just with you when he has afflicted you.

He has considered every angle, taken every factor into account. As he is to you, so he demands that you be with your children. He deplores impulsive outbursts based on inadequate information. Rather he demands that you inquire carefully and thoroughly and wherever possible (for he understands that you cannot be omniscient as he) that you satisfy every avenue of inquiry when serious discipline or punishment may be required.

Again his concern for justice is such that he never backs away from unpleasant issues, and he demands that we not back away either. It may at times seem judicious to turn a blind eye to things our children do, but we must never do so either because we ourselves fall short of God's standards or because we lack the courage to face our children's resentment. He calls us to be faithful to his just standards.

If in the previous chapter it seemed that we parents were getting off lightly, making do with what we had, it must now begin to be obvious that the demands on us are not less stringent than the books tell us, but more so. The more we think about God as our parent, the more we multiply responsibilities we have toward our children. The rule stands. As he is and has been to us, such are we called to be to our children.

You will notice that there is a difference between God's standard of parenting and human standards. His are infinitely more stringent. Nevertheless his demands are less grievous. The human instruction places you under an intolerable burden by making you responsible not only for your performance but for the results. God concerns himself primarily with your performance. He knows that while the results sometimes reflect your performance, they do not do so accurately. And when you fail, as you often will, he is patient and forgiving since he wants to teach you more about himself through the whole process of parenting.

If you follow human standards, the way is open both to pride and to despair since there is an implied cause-effect relationship between your performance and the results. On the one hand it can make you unjustifiably proud for your children may grow up respectably *in spite of your poor parental performance*. On the other hand if your children go badly astray in spite of conscientious parenting, you take all the blame and are given no way out.

Make it the aim of your life then to adopt God's standard and leave the results of doing so with him. Bring him your loaves and fishes telling him it is all you have, but look at what he demands you do with the loaves and fishes. It is not your responsibility to make sure five thousand stomachs are filled. It is your responsibility to obey instructions. Beside the Sea of Galilee, it meant to go on breaking and passing bread as long as the supply lasted. As a parent of growing children, it means that you will go on striving to be to your children all that God is to you. It is God's part to look after the miracles.

13
Dialog
with
Divinity

*I*t is not always easy to pray for our children. We know God listens. We know he cares. We know he answers. But often we don't feel like praying. What makes us reluctant to pray? Is it that God seems far away? That our prayers sound hollow and unreal?

The Roots of Reluctance

Sometimes we confuse faith with *feelings of faith*. The two are not the same. When we lack appropriate feelings (like the feeling that God is near or that prayer is a delight and a relief), we tend to lose heart. Our prayers seem to bounce back mockingly from the four walls.

God does not require feelings of faith nor should we strive to produce them. He does want faith, but faith is not a feeling so much as an attitude of our wills. By faith I defy my inner states and say, "I cannot feel you, Lord, but I know you are present and I know you can and will hear me." To pray like that is to begin to exercise faith. I should not look inside for appropriate feelings but at the invisible, unfelt God, and address my words to him by a defiant act of faith.

Reluctance might also arise from a vague sense of guilt, an inarticulate feeling that our prayers (as distinct from those of better Christians) will not be heard because they don't deserve to be. If so, our feelings deceive us. By all means we should confess the sins we know about and wish to abandon, and by all means we should be open to the Holy Spirit's conviction of specific sins. But if, as is so often the case, our prayers are hampered by an unfocused sense of uncleanness or unworthiness, then we are being fooled.

You and I have been made worthy. We have been adopted into God's family. Having acknowledged our sinfulness and having looked to Christ for redemption, we are complete in him. To be sure, our struggles against sin have often wound up in defeat. Nevertheless, provided we do not attempt to cover up or to pretend we are better than we actually are, our moral imperfections are taken care of by our redeemer.

If feelings of guilt arise (which may represent nothing more than mortification), we should ignore them and praise the Savior who made us worthy to enter the holiest place of all. We must lay aside false shame and remember that "if while we were enemies we were reconciled to God by the death of his Son, much more, now that we are reconciled, shall we be saved by his life" (Rom. 5:10).

Does grief inhibit prayer? God invites us to share our griefs with him. Some Christians feel that only praise, worship and expressions of confidence are acceptable to God. Yet grief, pain, suffering—all are a part of life and therefore may be a part of the traffic between God and you.

Hannah "was deeply distressed and prayed to the LORD, and wept bitterly" (1 Sam. 1:10). "Behold, O LORD, for I am in distress," cried Jeremiah, "my soul is in tumult, my heart is wrung within me.... Hear how I groan; there is none to comfort me" (Lam. 1:20-21). The Son of man himself sets us an example. "And he took with him Peter and James and John, and began to be greatly distressed and troubled. And he said to them, 'My soul is very sorrowful, even to death; remain here, and watch!' And . . . he fell on the ground and prayed" (Mk. 14:33-35).

Have you never groaned or wept before God? It is not right that your silence should rebuke the tender concern of the Most High, a God who listens and watches for the griefs of his people. Therefore you must not hide your grief because of mistaken notions about being spiritual or victorious. Are you more spiritual than the Son of man? If he needed to pour out his agony to the Father, then do you suppose it would be a weakness for you to do so?

Your sorrow, however, may be more than sorrow. Is there bewilderment as well as pain? You cannot understand perhaps how God could have failed to respond in the way you expected. You are torn by confusion and have to contend with bitterness and resentment toward him.

It is astonishing that the Lord high above all, the Creator of life and of time should pay gracious heed to our tiny resentments and frustrations. Yet he does. It constitutes no lack of reverence to confess to him how confused we feel at his failure to act like the God we thought we knew. Moreover, unless we do so, we shall never hear how he replies to our complaints.

Robbed of his children, scorned by his wife, debilitated by pain and sickness, and harassed by the trite criticisms of his friends, Job was stung into saying, "Only grant two things to me, then I will not hide myself from thy face: withdraw thy hand far from me, and let not dread of thee terrify me. Then call, and I will answer; or let me speak, and do thou reply to me" (Job 13:20-22).

Abraham was another man who challenged the ways of God, not out of conceit but out of distress and concern for the honor of God's name. "Wilt thou indeed destroy the righteous with the wicked? Suppose there are fifty righteous within the city; wilt thou then destroy the place and not spare it for the fifty righteous who are in it? Far be it from thee to do such a thing, to slay the righteous with the wicked, so that the righteous fare as the wicked! Far be that from thee! Shall not the Judge of all the earth do right?" (Gen. 18:23-25).

We could look at other examples of protest and questioning in God's presence, but one more is enough. In the horror of darkness and estrangement the crucified Jesus cried, "My God, my God, why hast thou forsaken me?"

So it is not wrong to come before God with a despairing *why*. It is better, much better to bring it to God than to turn it into a barrier that shuts God out. There is no better time to approach God than when we are bewildered and hurting. Should we fail to go to him, we may become feeble and twisted, bitter useless wrecks. But if we bring him our hurts and confusion, a number of things will happen. Our faith will deepen. Our minds and spirits will expand. We will have a larger capacity for living. We will become more free. Most important of all our knowledge and appreciation of God will grow.

The last few years have been painful years for my wife Lorrie and myself. It is impossible, of course, to estimate degrees of pain, and it is always easy to look around and find people whose pain exceeds ours. However, we found our own painful years difficult enough. Yet we would not be without them. The lessons we have learned are invaluable. Repeated pain has been a grim kind of training in developing certain attitudes and outlooks, and we have come to appreciate things about the person of God the Father that we never could have appreciated had it not been for the painful experiences we passed through.

Long-range Prayer

How should we pray for our children? What things ought we to ask for? How can we be sure our prayers will be heard?

To pray is to collaborate with God. It is to share his concern for our children and to bring his will to pass in their lives.

Obviously we cannot do this unless we know what his will is. Before we can begin to intercede effectively then, we must come to God with questions. "What are you trying to do in my child's life, Lord?"

"No longer do I call you servants," Jesus told his disciples, "for the servant does not know what his master is doing; but I have called you friends, for all that I have heard from my Father I have made known to you" (Jn. 15:15). We are his friends. We are those to whom in one degree or another he makes his will known. Many Christians continue all their lives in an infantile relationship with God. Like children, they ask for things they want. But we are to grow into adults in the family, adults who realize that many of the requests we made as children are now inappropriate. And as adults, we are to develop a growing concern about our Father's projects in the universe he rules and in our own households. Regarding our own children, he already has plans and projects for them. Our part is to collaborate with him. How may we know what his plans are?

We can know God's general plan for our children from Scripture. "For this is the will of God, your sanctification . . ." (1 Thess. 4:3). He wants our children to be holy. He wants them to become like his Son. So great is this desire that by his Holy Spirit he is actively working in their lives at this moment. We are called to work with him. He does not look on passively as we go about the struggle of rearing our children. Whether we see it or not, God is active. He invites us to help him.

While, as we saw before, God cannot and will not force our children into his kingdom, his Holy Spirit reveals the person of Christ in such a way that issues like sin, judgment and righteousness become powerfully clear. "And when he comes, he will convince the world concerning sin and righteousness and judgment" (Jn. 16:8). Our children need *to see such issues with absolute clarity.* There is no better hope nor prayer for them than that the nature of their need and the reality of the love of Christ should so dominate their consciousness that they will be in the best possible condition to make a true decision.

This, then, is the will of God for your children. His Son came to earth, and his Spirit now works to bring them enlightenment. We can pray for this enlightenment with absolute confidence.

God however, has even more specific goals for your children. He is concerned about their education, their future work, their health and their marital partners, to mention only a few things. Though it is hard for us to conceive that his mind could encompass so many details, nevertheless it does. How may we know the specifics of God's will?

Prayer does not begin with the repetition of names by rote. Some of the great prayers in the Bible were conceived over a period of time. Nehemiah, for instance, tells us he "sat down and wept, and mourned for days; and I continued fasting and praying before the God of heaven" (Neh. 1:4). Yet the prayer he records can be read aloud in a couple of minutes. Did Nehemiah repeat the prayer again and again for days on end? How do we account for the discrepancy between the length of the prayer he recorded and the length of time he tells us he spent in prayer?

There can be no doubt that the days of fasting and prayer were days when God was dealing with Nehemiah. The prayer he records is the end result of many days spent in wrestling with the problem before God. They were days of weeping, of bewilderment, days in which the Spirit of God was laying his finger on Nehemiah's own life. They were days during which Nehemiah's confusion turned to fear as God exposed him to ideas Nehemiah did not wish to entertain. Then came lucidity as he accepted God's will for him. In the end the only specific request he made was that God would protect him from the king's anger.

Like Nehemiah we must go to God with our problems and

wait in his presence. We are to express our concerns fully and to tell him of our bewilderment. We are to tell him, too, that we know he hears and that we cannot understand what is happening.

God never mocks people who approach him in this way. He is patient and gentle, and he takes his time. Occasionally he may clarify matters quickly, but more often the process is slow. God has aims in mind besides the well-being of our children. He wants to teach us about himself. The very problems we bring to him serve as the basis of a lesson, a lesson through which we will be changed, our view of him will become larger and the goal we are to seek for our children will be made clearer.

Understanding God's will involves more than intellectual apprehension. My heart has to be prepared, my outlook changed, my values adjusted, my knowledge of God's ways increased. Guidance by God differs radically from any other form of guidance. God invites me to enter into a deeper understanding, and at the same time challenges me about obedience to him. He seeks in these ways to raise me to be a true partner with him.

All this takes time, and cannot be hurried. In my panic I may want instant answers, but instant answers are usually valueless. God spent centuries turning Israel away from idol worship. Likewise, the pains I experience are to be turned to good account. Only as I grow and change am I able to grasp the nature of his will for my children. But I will come away from his presence with more than I ever asked for.

I do not know the nature of your trouble nor the amount of Christian experience you have. But I do know that God desires you to enter into a dialog with him. I cannot tell you how he will communicate with you, but I know both that he wants to and that he is capable of getting through any barrier to communicate his thoughts to you.

Take time. Don't hurry. Spread the matter out before the

Lord. Keep a Bible handy as you pray though not with the idea of receiving guidance like a horoscope reading. Rather it can help you recall godly principles you have forgotten or have been neglecting. Find the passages where the principles are explained. Write down how they specifically apply to your circumstances. As you do you will notice that the tumult in your heart is lessening. Something of God's quietness will bring a measure of peace. Slowly your view of a situation will begin to change, giving place to a new perspective, a changed outlook. You may begin to realize that certain things which seemed crucial are not as crucial as you thought, whereas others that you had not even considered now seem to be quite vital.

New objectives and long-range goals for your children will begin to formulate in your thinking. Commit them to prayer. Be wary of jumping too rapidly to conclusions. It is easy to mistake our own wishes for the will of God. Nevertheless, God who desires greatly that you share in his thoughts will help keep you from straying too far from a mistaken path.

Egg-shaped Requests
Many Christians feel uncomfortable about subjective guidance in prayer, and much that I have been saying concerns our subjective impressions. I certainly do not wish to suggest that your life be reoriented so that you commit your destiny to your whims and moods. But if God is to guide our praying about specific goals in our children's lives, then our subjective impressions will of necessity have to play a part. How can you be sure you are not being misled?

Let me reiterate. First, God wants to communicate with you more than you want to be communicated with. Second, his thoughts will be consistent with the highest ethical and moral standards, with God's way of doing things. Indeed the guidance may consist simply in following some scriptural principle.

Let me also suggest keeping a prayer diary. Many years ago I began recording details of the way God has led me in prayer as well as the precise nature of the requests I made. I also wrote in the date, leaving space to record subsequent happenings. It now makes startling reading, startling not only because of the dramatic and precise answers to prayer but because of some requests that I made which later proved badly mistaken. Though I am still not very wise, I am now a good deal wiser than I used to be about the ways of God.

Catherine Marshall in her book *Adventures in Prayer* mentions that she wrote the precise requests she made for each of her children's futures on a piece of paper the shape of an egg which she would then leave between the pages of her Bible. There was no magic in the method. The egg shape reminded her that prayers, like eggs, do not always hatch as soon as we lay them. If a sitting hen was to be preoccupied with the appearance of her eggs, unchanged and unchanging day after day, she would be very unhappy. We in a similar way tend to be unhappy if, having committed to God the requests which seem to be conformed to his will, we see no change. Prayers must mature before yielding their contents, and our impatience will do nothing to help.

You will, however, be tempted to pray repetitively, constantly demanding the same thing over and over again. It is as though by keeping the matter constantly active in your prayers you will make doubly sure that it will not find its way to the bottom of a heap of other people's requests or perhaps be filed by a heavenly clerk into an inactive drawer. It may dismay you perhaps to discover you have forgotten to pray for Jack's sanctification for a whole week and to realize simultaneously that Jack's sanctification now seems much less possible than it did when first you prayed about it. You feel as though you are losing ground in the battle to get the prayer pushed through and begin to agitate so that it gets proper priority.

We are not heard for our many words (Mt. 6:7-8). God is

not a busy executive with too many details to cope with. Yet what should we do once we have prayed and thought matters through? Do we then dismiss them from our minds? How should we regard the requests we have made while we are waiting for them to come to pass?

Certainly we should not forget them. If we entertain no doubts whatever that the requests will come to pass, then we should praise God constantly for what he will do. We praise because God is worthy to be praised and not because praise is a way of exerting pressure on God or of guaranteeing our hopes. Nor do we cease to praise and thank God once our prayers are answered, but must continue to praise him for past answers to prayer. If doubts do arise with the passage of time, we should bring the matter again before God, confessing our doubts and uncertainties asking for more wisdom.

Whatever doubts we may have about God's specific will in a problem, of one thing we should never be in doubt: God will give us wisdom when we ask him. He will meet us, hear us and continue to instruct us as we wait on him. "If any of you lacks wisdom, let him ask God, who gives to all men generously and without reproaching, and it will be given him" (Jas. 1:5).

Thus we may keep our requests active in our own minds. We do not allow ourselves to forget about our dealings with God. The lessons he teaches us must be kept alive in our daily thoughts so they will not be forgotten and so we will not slip back into old ways of looking at things. We do not keep them active so God will not forget (he neither will nor can) but for our own benefit. In this way we may sometimes find that we were too hasty about some requests whereas our conviction will continue to grow about others.

The "Prayer of Faith"
In some evangelical writings the virtues of what has been called "the prayer of faith" are extolled. Such a prayer will, it is said, always be answered.

The phrase is taken from James's epistle, "And the prayer of faith will save the sick man, and the Lord will raise him up" (Jas. 5:15). In its context the expression simply refers to prayer that is made believingly in the special circumstances James describes. It does not refer to a higher degree or order of faith applicable in a variety of situations. It is consistent with what Scripture elsewhere teaches, that believing prayer is answered.

I know of no Scriptures describing a special kind of prayer prayed with twenty-four-carat faith and am therefore hesitant to talk about the matter. However, there have been occasions in my life when I have known infallibly that my prayer has been heard and will be answered. I have compared notes with others who have enjoyed a similar experience.

But I must stress that the faith was not something I worked up into a special intensity. I have also found it to be an exception to my general experience in intercession. I do not attempt by manipulating my psyche to rise to the same degree of conviction about the majority of my requests. Most of the time I have to wrestle with doubts. If what I have experienced is what others call the prayer of faith, I can only say that the profound conviction that accompanied it was none of my doing. It was as though God had imparted a belief to me, as though he had surprised me by announcing very clearly what he was to do. No effort of faith on my part was called for. The only thing I could do was to say, "Amen! Blessed be God! So be it! Amen!" I do not believe that such experiences should be sought, nor do I regard them as a norm. It is much more important that we exercise ordinary faith, that is, that we adopt attitudes of mind and will as we learn to trust God. Faith is not the coin with which we barter for God's blessings. God waits to bestow blessings by sovereign grace, and faith "as a grain of mustard seed" is all he normally requires.

No Turning Back
When crises arise in the life of someone we are praying for, it

may try us as Christians far more than it would try an un-
believer. For the crisis may challenge all I believe about God.
It may seem to give the lie to the very things I have entrusted
to God. With a sinking heart I am tempted to think that my
prayers have all been self-deception.

It is important when your faith is badly shaken to wait until you have time to spend alone with God before you allow
yourself to wallow in despair. And when you do come to God,
the first thing you must remember is that he does not mock
his children. He is still there. His faithfulness has not wavered
a scrap. You may or you may not have misunderstood his will
and his intentions about one detail or another. But your mistake, if indeed it is a mistake, does not alter the basic situation.

Nehemiah underwent the painful shock of hearing of tragedy in Jerusalem even though prophets had clearly foretold
the city's restoration. Yet as he took his shattered faith into
the presence of God, the very crisis that had so shaken him was
the means of great blessing. Nehemiah became the leader of
Jerusalem's resurgence, developing in the process an intimate
relationship with God that is still moving to read.

I know a Canadian father who had long trusted God for his
sixteen-year-old son, a boy who had caused his parents great
pain. One night, after his son had traveled many hundreds of
miles from home to Vancouver, the father was gripped by a
sense of overwhelming sorrow that God should delay so long
in answering his prayers. He went into his study and closed
the door. Then falling on his face he reproached God bitterly.
"Do you not know what it feels like to be a human father?" he
asked. "Do you not care?"

Speaking about the matter later he said, "Then suddenly I
saw the compassion of God and my weeping became a weeping for joy and wonder." What had he seen? "It was like an
ocean with great waves heaving and crashing. But it wasn't an
ocean. It was the compassion of the heavenly Father heaving
and rolling endlessly in concern for us all." He said he lay for

many minutes weeping and praising God "for the glory he had seen."

In far away Vancouver at the very time he was praying, his son was also overwhelmed—but with conviction. Entering a church where a fellowship meeting was in progress, he was led to repentance and faith in Christ. "He still has a long way to go," the father said, "and the battle is not over by any means. But it's a different ball game now. We have turned a corner and there is no turning back."

The father's gratitude was for much more than his son's conversion. He had entered into an awareness of the glory of God's compassion to such a degree that the change in the boy seemed but a part of a greater whole.

In your own pain and tragedy you are being invited to enter into a close relationship with God. Whatever may or may not happen to your children, great good and enormous enrichment can come into your own life if only you will draw near to God. You may not enjoy unusual experiences or glory in visions, but your spirit can be set free. You can pass through fire and come out as fine gold. You can become more truly alive, more aware. Your very pain brings with it the possibility of untold riches.

Epilog

His wife was frowning and holding her head. As he sat on the edge of the bed watching her he wondered whether her headache and his own anxiety had a common cause.

"You worried about Jamie?"

"I guess." Pause. "I suppose that's what it must be."

She sighed. For some moments silence fell between them. It was his wife who broke it.

"Will it never end?"

He searched in his mind for comfort, but before he could think what to say she continued.

"I thought . . . I really thought we'd finally turned the corner. And you know I can't question that some of the good things that happened to him were genuine. I know he was trying. But now it's like we're back to square one."

Some months previously she had expressed both of their feelings when she had said, "I just can't take any more." Yet it seemed that events continued to batter them mercilessly whether they could "take it" or not.

"Hope deferred," the writer of the Proverbs tells us, "makes the heart sick" (13:12). Perhaps the most difficult emotional struggles parents face are not the early lacerations but the repeated reopening of half-healed wounds or the repeated uprootings of tender shoots of hope showing green promise on barren land. Many parents enjoy a happy ending to the story of their conflicts. It would be great if it could always be so. But the facts tell another tale. Some parents face lifelong disappointment.

Rejoice on Solid Rock
Some pin their hopes on the conversion of a troubled son or daughter and are overwhelmed with joy when the conversion takes place. And at times their joy holds. The conversion yields what it had promised and before their eyes a Christian character marvelously unfolds. At other times the results of the conversion, however genuine, are less satisfactory. Conversion and regeneration do not immediately and magically remove all character weaknesses, some of which demand long, continued responses to the Holy Spirit's discipline. A son's or a daughter's attitude may change radically and neither parent nor child should question the reality of what has taken place even if old habits begin to reassert themselves or old companions or temptations begin again to attract. Conflict does not end with conversion. Sometimes it may even intensify. Christians are nowhere promised immunity from temptation, nor does the enemy lightly yield his prey.

Other parents unconsciously pin their hopes on more tangible changes—the new job, the return to school, the responsibility of a promising marriage, a new set of friends, a new church affiliation. These changes and others must rightly be hailed with thanksgiving, yet the end may still not be in sight. How then shall Christian parents avoid being worn down by despair or bitterness? Where may they find a stable peace and hope which does not fail them?

Let me state the obvious. Place your hope in something

unstable and you can count on nothing. Circumstances are unpredictable. Future reactions of a son or daughter under stress cannot be foreseen with certainty. Hope built on anything so ephemeral as our subjective impression of current progress is a structure built on sand.

Faith rests ultimately not even on what God will do but on who God is. We may be mistaken about his future purposes and even more mistaken about what the future holds. But we need never be mistaken about who he *is*. He is faithful. He is compassionate. He is just. He is accessible.

There is sound logic then in Paul's injunction "Rejoice in the Lord always; again I will say, Rejoice" (Phil. 4:4). It is the first signpost on the road to parental peace. And if the road to which the signpost points should seem impossibly steep, take heart. It is far from impossible. Your first steps will be slow, and you may need to pause for breath from time to time. But by and by your legs will grow sturdy and your chest more expansile.

Since you cannot rejoice in the future, you must learn to rejoice in the Lord. Be clear what Paul is saying. He does not exhort us to be happy but to rejoice, which is quite different. Happiness may come or go. In a sense you have little control over it. There is no verb "to happy." Happiness is not something you can *do*. Joy on the other hand is. We can and should *rejoice*. That is to say, we can and should say with the prophet Habakkuk, "Though the fig tree do not blossom, . . . yet I will rejoice in the LORD, I will joy in the God of my salvation" (Hab. 3:17-18).

Whatever the exhortation to rejoice may seem to be, it is not a shallow cliché but a call to life and health. It is a call to detach our tendril hopes from crumbling walls in order to train them to climb solid rock.

We are governed by whatever dominates our attention. Read pornography all day and you will drool with lust. Read nothing but the tabloid press and you will become gullible.

Let your mind dwell on all the tragedies of your child's past and on all the possibilities of future ill, and your knees will shake and your heart turn to jelly.

You must be clear, however, that the Bible's command to rejoice is much more than a tip for psychological self-help. It is a call to reality, to a valid perspective. Peace (for the Christian) lies in the nature of reality itself, the total reality of a God-governed universe and the Christian's God-enclosed life. The command to rejoice *in the Lord* is a command to let a proportionate amount of our attention be occupied with reality's most basic fact: God.

It is likewise a call to faith, for the facts we perceive will at times seem in conflict with the goodness and power of God. "Does he really care? Has he not forgotten you? What made you think you deserved his help?" mocking voices from the pit will gleefully demand. At such a time our rejoicing in the Lord may have to begin as we firmly reply, "It is written! It is written! It is written!"

The very foundation of our faith is at stake. Was Jesus in fact born of a virgin? Did he rise from the dead? Does he plead for us before the majesty on high? For if such things are true then let circumstances seem what they may, our hope rests on secure foundations.

Look again at Habakkuk's cry of triumph in the last three verses of his prophecy. Having seen the awful nature of God's ultimate judgment upon his foes, the prophet is in terror of God so great that in verse 16 he decides to sit down and wait patiently for God to vindicate his name. Yet now as he looks around at what once were evidences for despair and at the terrible threat of famine (v. 17), the realization breaks over him that tragic as the picture may be, it no longer matters. The universe is on a solid footing. God will be God and Habakkuk's voice ringingly asserts his joy in the fact. His shaking of verse 17 gives place to strength and agility in verse 19. The last glimpse we catch is of a prophet leaping like a mountain goat up the face of steep rocks. The signpost labeled "Rejoice!" commands you however impossible it may seem to follow.

The Practice of the Present

There is a second signpost labeled "Do not be anxious about tomorrow" (Mt. 6:34). I am, to be sure, taking the words out of their context which has to do with anxiety about our material needs. But I am not doing violence to them. Jesus is applying a general rule about anxiety to a specific situation, and it is to the general rule I wish to call attention. "Do not be anxious about tomorrow, for tomorrow will be anxious for itself. Let the day's own trouble be sufficient for the day." Nowadays we express something similar when we advise people to "live a day at a time." It is sound advice. After all we can live only a day at a time. But I prefer the way Jesus puts it.

We need our second signpost if we are to learn to leap rather than struggle along an uphill road. Since the future is unknown and since we, like nature, abhor a vacuum, we fill it with imagined hopes and fears which bear little relationship to the future's true content. We have already looked at the treachery of entertaining false hopes for the future. In the case of fears we should note their futility. We torture ourselves with terrors that will never come to pass, wasting agony on mere fantasy.

As Christians we are called to live primarily in the present. We are to think about today; not tomorrow, but today. Today we have duties to perform. Today we may reach out and touch God. Tomorrow has not yet arrived, but today has. There may not even be a tomorrow. But today is a gift placed in our hands, a gift we can only use if we keep ourselves from being distracted by tomorrow.

Admittedly we must not take the principle to such an extreme that we close our eyes to those responsibilities for today that bear on the future. But the problem most parents face is of being overwhelmed by the future, paralyzed with the dread of what tomorrow may bring. For such a state of mind there is only one valid piece of advice: today's problems are enough for today.

> God holds the key of all unknown,
> And I am glad;
> If other hands should hold that key
> Or if He trusted it to me
> I might be sad.
>
> What if tomorrow's cares were here,
> Without its rest?
> I'd rather He unlocked the day.
> And, as the hours swing open, say,
> "My will is best."[1]

Living in the present is, however, a disciplined art that has to be learned. It can only become a habit of mind if it is practiced constantly over months, even years. Nor should it be regarded, any more than the matter of rejoicing in the Lord, as a bit of psychological uplift. To be sure it makes good psychological sense. However, it is also a Christian duty. The Christian who assumes too much responsibility for the future is presumptuous. He assumes the prerogatives of omnipotence and omniscience, trying to nudge the Almighty aside, bidding him make room for him on his throne. Now it is one thing to be seated with Christ in heavenly places, but it is quite another to forget which seat belongs to us and which seat belongs to the Father.

To live in the present is to acknowledge that we are creatures and that God is God. The discipline then is not just of service to us but of honor to God. We are not merely advised to learn it but commanded to do so.

Living in the present also implies enjoying today's pleasures. If you feel no pleasures exist for you today, you may not have been keeping your eyes open. I used to collect wild-flowers, those explosions of delicate beauty that the Creator flings like confetti over the hedgerows and woods. I never realized how many there were till I started looking. I would find a strange happiness as I searched for rare ones. A new music would begin inside me. We are surrounded, anywhere, anytime by little beauties. A pleasing sound, the changing skies, starlight, snow crystals, birdsong, the changing seasons. We need to form the habit of looking and seeing, of listening and hearing and of pausing to savor and enjoy.

Wildflowers may not do for you what they did for me, but there are treasures, little treasures for you too, whatever your taste may be. You will have to drop some of your cares and take time to look if you want to enjoy them.

O what is life, if, full of care
We have not time to stand and stare?

One mother wrote me, "I started a *joy* box which was a collection of . . . cartoons and letters and poems and anything that brought me back to reality." I cannot state that savoring life's little treasures is a duty. Yet it is more than a psychological self-help. (And as a psychiatrist I am deeply suspicious of mere mood manipulation.) It reveals a wholesome attitude to life. If you should find yourself incapable of enjoying little treasures even though you are looking out for them, then you would be advised to seek professional help.

The Fellowship of Pain

A third and final signpost reads, "Do not grieve alone." There must be someone, somewhere with whom you can share your pain. Find that someone. I know that you may have shared your pain with God. However, I speak of a fellow human. I agree that not everyone will want to share your burden. You may question your right to share it. Yet Christian fellowship exists, among other things, for the sharing of pain and of pleasure. Pain shared is pain divided. Pleasure shared is pleasure multiplied. Therefore Christian fellowship, where it is a true sharing-praying fellowship, can be a resource of incalculable value.

I suppose there is a sense in which our suffering contributes to the well-being of the fellowship, especially if we have been able to discover God's help in our pain. "Blessed be ... the Father of mercies and God of all comfort," writes Paul, "who comforts us in all our affliction, so that we may be able to comfort those who are in any affliction, with the comfort with which we ourselves are comforted by God" (2 Cor. 1:3-4).

Why do you think I wrote this book? I have not written as a psychiatrist to readers who might benefit from my professional knowledge but as a parent who has tasted the bitterness of despair and found a larger God as a result of groping in the darkness. It is an invitation to join the fellowship of parents in pain—or better, a fellowship of parents who through pain have grasped the hand of a larger, more powerful and more tender God than ever we knew existed.

Notes

Chapter 2
[1]Margaret Mead, *From the South Seas* (New York: Morrow, 1936).
[2]D. W. Goodwin et al., "Alcohol Problems in Adoptees Raised apart from Alcoholic Biological Parents," *Archives of General Psychiatry,* 28 (1973), 238; 31 (1974), 164-69.
Chapter 3
[1]Derek Kidner, *Proverbs: An Introduction and Commentary* (Downers Grove, Ill.: InterVarsity Press, 1964), p. 51.
[2]Ibid.
[3]C. S. Lewis, *Surprised by Joy* (New York: Harcourt, Brace & World, 1955), p. 229.
[4]John White, *The Fight* (Downers Grove, Ill.: InterVarsity Press, 1976), p. 113.
Chapter 5
[1]Konrad Z. Lorenz, *On Aggression* (New York: Bantam, 1967), pp. 111-16, 140.
Chapter 7
[1]John White, *Eros Defiled* (Downers Grove, Ill.: InterVarsity Press, 1977), pp. 105-39.
[2]Alex Davidson, *The Returns of Love* (Downers Grove, Ill.: InterVarsity Press, 1970).
Chapter 10
[1]Richard Farsen, "The Technology of Humanism," *Journal of Humanistic Psychology,* 18, No. 2 (Spring 1978).
Chapter 12
[1]Francis Foulkes, *The Epistle of Paul to the Ephesians* (Grand Rapids, Mich.: Eerdmans, 1963), pp. 101-02.
[2]Mary Shekleton, "It Passeth Knowledge," *Hymns* (Downers Grove, Ill.: InterVarsity Press, 1952), 133.
Epilog
[1]J. Parker, "God Holds the Key," *Hymns of Truth and Praise* (Fort Dodge, Iowa: Gospel Perpetuating Publishers, 1971), 528